Paper Dolls

Paper Dolls

HOW TO FIND, RECOGNIZE, BUY, COLLECT, AND SELL THE CUTOUTS OF TWO CENTURIES

Anne Tolstoi Wallach

with photographs by peter bosch

VAN NOSTRAND REINHOLD COMPANY

NEW YORK CINCINNATI TORONTO LONDON MELBOURNE

Copyright © 1982 by Anne Tolstoi Wallach
Library of Congress Catalog Card Number 81-10444
ISBN 0-442-20046-3

Printed in the United States of America
Designed by Dana Kasarsky Design

Published by Van Nostrand Reinhold Company Inc.
135 West 50th Street
New York, NY 10020

Van Nostrand Reinhold Limited
1410 Birchmount Road
Scarborough, Ontario M1P 2E7, Canada

Van Nostrand Reinhold Australia Pty. Ltd.
17 Queen Street
Mitcham, Victoria 3132, Australia

Van Nostrand Reinhold Company Limited
Molly Millars Lane
Wokingham, Berkshire, England

16 15 14 13 12 11 10 9 8 7 6 5 4 3 2 1

Library of Congress Cataloging in Publication Data

Wallach, Anne Tolstoi.
Paper dolls, how to find, recognize, buy,
collect, and sell the cutouts of two centuries.

Bibliography: p.
Includes index.
1. Paper dolls. I. Title.
NK4894.A2W34   745.592′21   81-10444
ISBN 0-442-20046-3   AACR2

Acknowledgments

To the collectors: Joan Carol Kaltschmidt, Jean Woodcock, Betsy Slap,
Barbara Jendrick, Mary Young, Marta Krebs, Jan and Larry Malis,
Jo Ann Reisler, Phyllis Salak, Tim and Betsy Trace, Jonathan
and Barbara Newman, K. Gregory, Janie Varsolona, Louise Kaufman,
Joyce McClelland, Elsie Stevens, Zelda Cushner, Rose-Marie Collins,
Paula Hill, Virginia Crossley, and the others who wrote, taught, shared
and helped.

To Felicia Eth, who believed in the project from the start; Mabel Cram,
who checked it out; Max Sirota, who helped design it; and Maggie Noble,
who tidied it up.
And to my husband, who remained patient and encouraging throughout.

Contents

Paper Dolls

Introduction

What is a paper doll? The *Random House Dictionary* states cautiously, "A paper or cardboard, usually two-dimensional, representation of the human figure, used as a child's toy."

Yet there are paper dolls that make use of fabric, plywood, and plastic. There are three-dimensional paper dolls, dolls to thread for making jumping jacks, dolls that wear wrap-around clothing, dolls that fold into standing models. There are paper dolls that represent ducks, teddy bears, Kewpies, brownies, even pigs, all with changeable paper clothing. And paper dolls did not begin or end as toys for children.

Then what *is* a paper doll? If you are a woman past thirty, paper dolls mean the flat pictures you cut out as a child and dressed in paper clothes that were attached by tabs. You bought yours at the local five-and-ten-cent store, cut them out of your mother's magazines, and probably designed extra fashions for the ones you loved most. If you are under thirty, paper dolls may

seem to you a kind of antique, like a Mickey Mouse watch or a 1939 World's Fair souvenir. They have the fascination of old fashion engravings or thrift-shop clothing. Or you may have loved them as a child yourself, for simple punch-out paper dolls are still sold today.

What can paper dolls mean to you now? If you are an artist, paper dolls offer a history of illustration available in no other source as accessible, carefully dated, or intimate. If the history of fashion intrigues you, paper dolls offer a course in the changing trends of dress for men, women, and children over the past two hundred years. In addition to the suits, coats, and dresses you can see in costume museums, paper dolls will show you accurate pictures of the underwear, headgear, and shoes appropriate to each fashion, articles not so easily found in costume collections because they were more perishable then precious outerwear.

If you are interested in the development of printing techniques, pa-

per dolls illustrate a two-century range, from engraving through lithography to high-speed newspaper press runs. When you handle paper dolls, you not only see the differences in these reproduction methods, you can feel the differences, and understand how papers' textures are used to enhance the designs.

If you love the past, paper dolls give you the satisfaction of holding a part of it, genuine and beautiful, which might crumble into rubbish unless you chose to preserve it. Paper dolls form a record, precise and personal, of the social changes of two centuries. They illustrate the attitudes and interests of women and children in a form that is readily grasped and understood.

Popular men and women of different eras and nations are easy to see and contrast when you hold them in your hand as paper dolls: Kaiser Wilhelm is preserved with a selection of handsome military uniforms, Jacqueline Kennedy is represented with a wardrobe from her White House years. Almost every celebrity of stage, movies, politics, royalty, childrens' fiction, and fashion exists in paper-doll form.

Paper dolls clearly display the accessories that belong with a woman's art deco winter suit, or the sporting activities a 1911 man of fashion would be equipped to play. They illustrate the layette a baby might have worn at the turn of the century, the changing stockings women have worn for two centuries, the history of hats for men and women. Paper dolls record accurately the service uniforms of the women's army and navy during World War II, the movie wardrobes of top Hollywood stars, the Depression fashions of America's 1930s, the clothes worn by England's princesses Elizabeth and Margaret Rose as children; they show the gowns of the wives of American presidents, the peasant costumes of Europe, the outfits of Chinese and Japanese royalty.

If your interest is primarily collecting paper dolls for fun and profit, you should know that this is just beginning as an organized activity, and you can easily get in on the ground floor. Paper dolls provide a body of material you can buy for very little money, or even amass for no money at all. You can sell your collection quickly, whenever you choose, at prices that have risen quite steadily almost every month over the last ten years, and show no signs of stabilizing.

If you would like an area of expertise, to know more about one subject than most people know, paper dolls are a field in which almost every collector starts even. Nobody has yet found and cataloged all the paper dolls ever made. There is no sign yet of the catalog raisonné, the accurate, descriptive grouping of all paper dolls. Experts who have been collecting for years are still puzzled over certain dates and provenances, still disagree over which hat belongs with which costume. Material

comes to light almost every time an attic is turned out or an old warehouse torn down. The history of paper dolls is still being written, and there is a chance for you to contribute to it. A group of dedicated collectors exists in the United States, a group which selflessly shares information and pictures to increase the body of knowledge. You can find a paper doll in one minute which can catapult you into expertise, if none of the experts has seen that particular doll before.

Paper dolls have not been researched for long, nor have they been studied by scholars. Until about fifteen years ago, they were regarded as rubbish by all but a small group of collectors. Museums in the United States and Europe have preserved a few examples from the eighteenth and nineteenth centuries, but seldom display them except on special occasions, since the dolls are fragile and difficult to show. Antique dealers have bypassed paper dolls for the same reasons, and because until recently there has been little profit in handling them.

The few people who have loved and gathered paper dolls for years have corresponded zealously with one another, piecing bits of history together and exchanging news about their own collections. Several of them have organized newsletters and magazines devoted to paper dolls and to identifying and illustrating paper-doll material. Some collectors have privately printed identification books and careful studies of certain groups of paper dolls. But no one has yet recorded a history of paper dolls as a body of material, or discussed why they began when they did, flourished as they did and died out as a popular pastime.

This book aims to give a general account, based only on material that exists to be seen or held in the hand, not on guesswork, sentiment, or secondhand description. Unfortunately, some collectors with the best

intentions have passed on the same myths and mistakes. While some paper dolls have been described, redrawn, and identified down to the smallest detail, others have been almost totally ignored.

Later research will certainly add to the information here and fill in details, because so much is left to learn. Today's collectors can easily augment parts of this history from their own material; yesterday's collectors have already supplied us with identification books and checklists. This overall look at paper-doll history is an outline, ready to encompass additional discoveries. It does not attempt to include every detail, nor are the illustrations in complete groups, but rather, examples of main currents of style.

Above all, this history links paper dolls to their times. Sensible speculation can fill in gaps. It should be clear why nineteenth-century children in all Western countries played passionately with paper toys, why the golden age of paper dolls was during the Depression of the 1930s, and why paper dolls died when television was born.

Most people understand that a paper doll is a flat picture of a figure, designed to back a changeable group of costumes. And most people recognize the little paper tabs used to hold the clothes to the figure, although those tabs came late and are not the only way to dress a paper doll. But even men and women who have never seen a paper doll close-up still understand the idea perfectly. When *Time* magazine illustrated the many roles of Henry Kissinger in the Nixon administration with a cartoon paper doll, readers understood the meaning. When a modern artist creates "clayper" dolls of flat sculpture with ceramic tabs, as Ellie Fernald did in 1977, people recognize the form.

Even the language of paper dolls is still with us. If a writer refers to paper-doll politicians, we understand that in the writer's opinion they will not perform as well as real, three-dimensional statesmen. When a popular song refers to the need for a paper doll we can call our own, everyone grasps the sentiment.

But any history of paper dolls will mean most to people who played with them as children. If you were one, you probably remember your favorites. You will certainly recognize them when you find them in this book. If you carried your dolls to friends' houses to share, if you made extra dresses for your best dolls, if you bought two and even three of the same sets so you could own a favorite forever, you are a potential adult collector. Most collectors began as children, and still mourn the paper dolls their mothers tossed out. And most collectors begin alone, convinced they are the only ones in the world who could be interested in such trivia. All are delighted to discover that paper dolls fascinate a great number of adult men and women, and are vigorously bought and sold all over America and Europe.

These pleasures used to belong only to the collectors of "real" dolls. But prices have risen so fast and so far that few people can buy back their childhood favorites today. The Shirley Temple you owned as a little girl now sells for $400 or $500, and even an early Barbie of the 1950s can cost $30 or more. It is much less expensive to search for your childhood again in paper and to find your paper dolls in exactly the same uncut condition in which you first spotted them at your local five-and-ten. Paper-doll collectors can go home again.

You can begin by just simply turning the pages of this book and looking at the pictures. Even if you had the best collection on your block, you will be surprised by the scope and history of the paper-doll world.

part one
The History of Paper Dolls

Origins

There has been much speculation among collectors about the precise beginnings of paper dolls, but if we look at three separate records we can make an educated guess about how and when paper dolls emerged as playthings. These records are the history of paper, the history of toys, and the records of existing paper dolls.

The history of paper dolls obviously begins after the invention of paper. This is believed to have taken place in China in A.D. 105, when a blend of pressed pulp replaced the bamboo and silk on which Han scholars had written until then.

Paper moved with traders to Japan by the seventh century, and to the Middle East by the eighth century. The first paper mill in the Moslem world was established in Samarkand in 751. The Moors brought paper into Spain by the twelfth century; its use spread to France, where the first mill in Christian Europe was established in 1189. Until that time scholars and churchmen wrote and drew on parchment sheets. By 1494 the first

paper mill was built in England, and by 1689 the first American mill was in operation at Germantown, Pennsylvania. Not until 1807, when the Fourdrinier press improved papermaking to a point that was profitable for mass sales, did paper become a common household article, and only then could it be used for making children's toys.

The history of toys also suggests that paper dolls could not have been possible before the middle of the eighteenth century. Miniature objects have existed all through history, but most were religious objects, like the Egyptian figures found in tombs, or the precious possessions of wealthy adults. The Greeks and Romans gave their children simple toys, like balls, dolls, and tops, which we know from contemporary vase paintings and literature. In Europe throughout the Middle Ages there are few indications that toys other than the simplest ones existed at all; Breughel's painting of children's games shows only balls, hoops, and tops. In 1614 Ben Jonson wrote

about the toys and miniatures for children sold at Bartholomew Fair, and these probably came from German woodcarvers, who began their toymaking somewhat earlier. It took another century for Horace Walpole and the Reverend Woodforde, writing accounts of daily life, to mention toys at all. Parson Woodforde refers to a paper caravan costing one and sixpence.

Most toys left for us to see, like the beautiful dollhouses in Amsterdam's Rijksmuseum or the Neapolitan crèches shown in many museums at Christmas, are not really toys. Even most dolls preserved from the eighteenth century were used as fashion models, and were too precious to be given to children. Before the eighteenth century, European children were treated like small adults: poor ones went to work at early ages, and rich ones were educated from the ages of three and four, spending long hours over their books, weapons, and domestic equipment.

Until children were allowed time and equipment for play there could be no paper dolls, and even wooden dolls from the seventeenth century are rare. It took the eighteenth century to provide leisure, money, and the spirit for giving children time and toys of their own. By the 1760s there were toyshops in London, selling articles made of various natural materials, of which paper was one of the most popular.

Collectors have long accepted the idea that Marco Polo brought paper dolls from China to Europe in the thirteenth century. But though religious figures made of paper and bark existed in China, Japan, and South America, they were not toys, nor are they related to modern paper dolls.

Another favorite legend about the origin of paper dolls tells they were created along with Italian commedia dell'arte. Though there are many movable figures of the Harlequins, Columbines, and Scaramouches of that theatrical tradition, there is no evidence that any were made before the eighteenth century.

Both the history of paper and the history of playthings point to the mid-eighteenth century as the time when paper dolls were first possible. By 1750 the costs of paper and printing had reached a point where upper-class children could have printed books or pictures. By then, too, children had begun to have time for play. The true record of paper dolls thus dates from about 1750.

The first paper dolls used for amusement appear to have come from the court of Louis XV, where Madame de Pompadour, and later Madame du Barry, led the fashionable world in a constant search for new baubles and amusements. Puppets and fashion dolls were in vogue at the court; a French writer of 1747 notes that the Duchesse de Chartres paid 1,500 *livres* for a puppet painted by Boucher. No doubt, less extravagant ladies turned to puppets made of paper.

These paper puppets, pieces of which were cut out, strung together, and made to move, were called *pantins* in France, probably because many were made in the Parisian suburb of that name. Other countries have different names for these figures, suggesting that their popularity spread to the aristocracy of different courts. In Germany they were called *Hampelmenn,* in Italy *fanucci,* in England jumping jacks. The *pantin* is the ancestor of all activated paper dolls; early ones are scarce and most are in museums. Favorite subjects included commedia dell'arte figures, shepherds, and milkmaids, and veiled caricatures of court personalities. The generalized figures were no doubt safer in the changing political climate at Versailles.

In France, the Pellerin family of Epinal, which had produced pictures on paper for almost a century before, created *pantins* with woodblocks and primitive dye colors. While the bulk of the family's work, known as Images d'Epinal, appeared in later centuries, the tradition began around 1800.

Pantins have often been reproduced. Reproductions are always carefully labeled and are always on cleaner, heavier paper than originals, so they are easy to recognize. Costume research fixes most originals at about 1770 or later, despite the claims of some museums to have seventeenth-century *pantins.* Jumping jacks of different materials have been known since early history, as have marionettes, which are related to these moving figures. But paper *pantins* are not known to have existed before the eighteenth century.

A similar adult toy was popular at court as a love token. Small notes were painted on parchment in delicate watercolor, showing ladies and gentlemen in costumes or activities that changed as the cards opened. These notes show an early use of paper for a visual trick. There were

others; early prints with views painted on mica—a thin, transparent material—were laid over each other to change the pictures. Prints with cutout areas to be backed by fabrics or other pictures date from the sixteenth century. These playthings for adults helped develop the paper doll as we know it; a figure changed by the addition of a second layer of paper.

The French Revolution temporarily ended the privileges and playthings of the aristocracy, and scattered most examples of their toys. When nobles fled the Terror they took jewels and gold, leaving toys behind. Most of their playthings were lost to history.

But the trick picture—an original with an overlay made to fool the eye (*tromper l'oeil* in French)—survived. In France it was quickly adopted as a business tool by the rising middle class. Paper dolls were used as dressmaker's and milliner's samples, as well as advertisements for actresses, who change clothes with their roles, and for prostitutes, who remove their clothes altogether. Early paper dolls of nude figures are museum-quality examples, originally meant for gentlemen to carry and display discreetly, not for children's play.

From the few paper dolls of this period came the inspiration for many later dolls and toys. Paper heads were used as the bases for varieties of paper hats, probably milliner's samples. Many handmade paper dress samples flourished in conjunction with the first magazines devoted solely to fashion, which appeared in England in the late 1700s. Cutout and colored paper was more suitable for fashion illustration than flat black and white. The cost and detail of the earliest examples leave little doubt that they were adults' toys, not children's.

As the samples spread about, so did the idea of paper designed for children. Daughters of wealthy women who had paper dressmaker's samples probably seized on them for their own. From the late eighteenth century on, there was a burst of paper toys meant specifically for boys and girls. German engravers used great skill in creating regiments of paper soldiers, animals, houses, furniture, peep shows, panoramas, and theaters. These were cheaper than other toys and easier to copy at home. In England and France trick paper books silhouettes, and other devices for making "moving" pictures appeared rapidly. Boys and girls from well-to-do families in England and on the Continent were enchanted with paper toys. Paper was relatively costly, and scissors were precious objects meant for fine sewing and cutting fabric. A girl who owned a pair of scissors was expected to keep it, often chained to her belt, throughout childhood, like a piece of fine jewelry. Scissor grinders preserved these instruments, which were often made of silver and gold and beautifully decorated. Since scissors were too valuable to be used for toys, many early paper dolls were precut. Early paper dolls were either handmade or hand-colored engravings. Though labor was cheap in the eighteenth century, fine workmanship went into their production, and they were not inexpensive for their times. As the demand for these toys grew, so did the need for new ideas to make them interesting and salable. The pictures began to show items from the daily lives of the children to whom they would be sold. This is the start of the fascinating record of popular culture visible throughout paper-doll history.

Without exception, paper dolls that can be dated before 1800 are rare and precious. Your chances of finding any in flea markets or antique shops are equally rare. The intrinsic worth of these dolls is clear even to a novice, making bargain purchases improbable. However, in the world of paper dolls almost any discovery is possible. Antique paper dolls have been found between the pages of old books or tucked into old sewing boxes. Throughout history, children have stored their paper dolls in flat places, so surprises abound.

If you want to own a very early paper doll you will be more likely to find one in the pages of a rare-book catalog, or in the stock of a dealer in ephemera (old paper objects meant to be thrown away), or by searching out a dealer in old children's books. These dolls will be costly, some as high as thousands of dollars. Although high, the prices will be worth paying as investments, because growing interest has sent prices for all paper dolls higher every year for some time. The early dolls are little works of art, never to be repeated. A French dressmaker's sample from 1789 and her wardrobe were bought from a rare-book dealer in 1978 for $350. While this may seem expensive for a paper toy, the same amount would purchase little enough in most collecting fields. In the following year the same doll, called Miss Lascelles, brought offers for more than twice the amount. Few other fields offer such rewarding price rises in so short a time.

Early paper dolls are unique, beautiful designs on marvelous paper with a special look and feel, executed in enduring colors by skillful hands. Each is an individual treasure, a small mirror of its time and world. To own one is to hold a part of the past in your hand.

2
The First Hundred Years

By 1800, printing in large impressions had become inexpensive enough so that the middle class could afford books and pictures. In 1810, Friedrich Koenig applied steam power to the printing press. While the quality of printing did not change, the quantity was greatly increased, and the cost of each page lowered. Common people in England and on the Continent began to buy paper books and prints. Soon they began to buy them for children.

The trick paper toy had been brought to England from France by aristocrats fleeing the revolution. Curiously, paper dolls as business tools continued in use in France, while paper dolls as toys flourished in England. This was probably because the French middle class was eager to develop new commercial techniques.

In 1810, the year of Napoleon's greatest power, a London printer, S. and J. Fuller, produced a small book in a cardboard slipcase called *The History of Little Fanny Exemplified in a Series of Figures*. Sold at the Temple of Fancy, an outlet for games and toys, it was an instant success, and set the pattern for many paper dolls to follow.

The few children's books of this time were moral tales or instructions in manners. Writers like Maria Edgeworth sugar-coated their messages in story form, though they were still messages, not purely entertainment. *Little Fanny* went a step farther in adding play value by illustrating the heroine and her changes of fortune in paper-doll form.

Little Fanny tells the story of a naughty child who runs away from home with beggars, has a series of adventures, and returns home, having learned her lesson. The immense popularity of the book can be seen from the fact that in 1810 Fuller printed at least six editions. More followed in England, and the book was quickly pirated by European publishers. Fuller soon brought out a matching book, *The History and Adventures of Little Henry*, another fanciful tale about a small boy stolen by gypsies.

Fuller continued to bring out these chapbooks, each with hand-colored cut figures, no two precisely alike. The form of the dolls—paper heads on bars to be fitted into the costumes—probably evolved from *pantins* with their movable heads and limbs. Subsequent books used characters called Young Albert; Lauretta, the little Savoyard; Ellen, or the naughty girl reclaimed; and Phoebe, the cottage maid. All of them sold well to English parents.

Continental printers not only copied the Fuller books but also, encouraged by their sales, quickly brought out versions of their own. In France a little book called *Frédéric ou les Effets de la Désobéissance* appeared, a fable copied almost directly from *Little Henry*. The Dutch followed with the adventures of Runaway Willem, in the same form.

The Fuller books sold in England for six shillings, a considerable amount for a toy at the time; the Continental books were comparably priced. These prices were high

for ordinary people, and many middle-class mothers evidently borrowed copies and wrote the stories out. Handwritten and hand-drawn copies turn up from time to time, many even more charming than the printed originals.

The Fuller books established more than a format for a story with paper figures: they set the pattern for the idea of paper as a children's toy, worth a fair sum and worth preserving. This is the reason you can still find originals in good condition, complete with costumes, in antiquarian bookshops or antique stores. *Little Fanny* and *Little Henry* are recognizably works of art, not paper trash. They are easier to buy today than many cheaper, flimsier paper dolls of a later era which were automatically discarded as rubbish.

The Germans were the first to develop a paper-doll form that would cost considerably less than the precut Fuller books, and thus achieve wider sales. Flat sheets called *Bilderbogen* ("picture sheets") were meant to be cut out by children. They added to paper-doll play the cutting

out itself, which is so much a part of the dolls' appeal (although the flat sheets can be admired in themselves). Cutting is an activity with a little suspense and danger to it, since a slip can spoil a design. The complete wardrobe of a paper doll is partly the work of its cutter, and so more dear to the owner. Eager children cut out their favorite costumes first; cautious ones practiced on less interesting costumes and saved the best for last. Partially cut sheets found more than a century later testify to the method.

Printed sheets from Germany came large and small, the earliest dating from about 1845. They were designed for play alone, not for moral instruction of any kind. Play was recognized as a worthwhile activity in itself, a big step in social attitudes toward children. Many of the *Ankleidepuppen* ("dress-up dolls") appeared in series form, some in beautifully decorated folders, which grew fancier as time went on. The color of the sheets is crude, but the detail of the drawings shows the level of skill and patience

Ellen, or the Naughty Girl Reclaimed, a Story Exemplified in a Series of Figures (1811) was one of several successful paper-doll books published by S. and J. Fuller, London. Like *Little Fanny* and *Little Henry,* all the figures are hand colored, with no two exactly alike.

A large sheet of *Ankleidepuppen* ("dress-up dolls"), Germany, c. 1845. The costumes and accessories are detailed and varied, requiring skillful cutting.

expected from nineteenth-century children. No little girl could have cut out the tiny ribbons, lace edgings, and butterfly nets of these sheets unless she had been taught cutting and stitching at an early age.

Paper dolls form a record of what was expected of children in different times. The Fuller books, moral stories made more attractive by paper toys, belong to their time and place, and no other. The German sheets tell us that children were expected to play quietly and neatly, working nimbly with precise motions.

By the middle of the nineteenth century another kind of record begins to appear in paper dolls—the record of the celebrity. Before the nineteenth century, except for a few members of royalty or the artistic community, the idea of an international celebrity was unknown. The small groups of educated people in each country were still too isolated from one another to share the appreciation of any single contemporary. But with the Industrial Revolution, as news traveled faster and travel itself became cheaper, the first international stars appeared.

The earliest celebrity paper dolls were based on theatrical people, probably because they moved from city to city, and because they assumed the different roles which made them suitable for costume changes. Printers were eagerly seeking new ideas for designs; with so many family and fashion dolls, the celebrity doll was a publishing event.

Lucile Grahn, called the first dancer of London, exists as a paper doll represented only by a box cover. At this time paper dolls were being presented in beautiful wooden and cardboard boxes, gilded and decorated, collector's items themselves.

Maria Taglioni, an enormously popular dancer of the 1840s, was the model for the first doll known to have been printed in several sizes

sold at different prices. The costumes illustrated many of her most famous roles. An original is in the collection of the Museum of the City of New York.

Fanny Elssler, a Viennese ballerina, also modeled for a magnificent paper doll set of the 1840s. This set was quickly followed by one designed after the most popular singer of her day, Jenny Lind. The Lind set was published with the consent of the star, the figure drawn from her favorite portrait. Each costume showed one of her operatic roles, plus a gown for concerts. The set was meant to encourage children's love for music.

These dolls were all colored by hand, so that no two are exactly alike. The size varied from about four inches to nine; therefore they reached a wider audience than the Fuller books, because the smallest sizes were not expensive. A few black-and-white reproductions have been printed by the museums which own the originals, and even these copies are now rare. The originals are few, their prices high. They are probably the most sought-after examples of paper dolls.

Interest in paper dolls was also growing in America. Publishers in New York and Boston saw the profits to be made from bigger editions made to sell at lower prices than the European boxed sets. In 1854 a Boston printer, Crosby, Nichols & Company, produced an American version of *Little Fanny*. It was called *Fanny Gray* and combined English-style storybook figures and a European-style decorated box. The reading matter was a verse account of the ups and downs of Fanny's life, from orphan to match girl to reclamation by her uncle, but the tone is less didactic than Fuller's and the dolls are larger and more colorful. *Fanny Gray* rapidly became as popular in America as her predecessor had been in England. The lithography for the set was by S. W.

Chandler & Brothers, a family whose descendant, Herbert Hosmer, Jr., today maintains the John Greene Chandler Memorial in South Lancaster, Massachusetts, where much of the original Chandler material can be seen. *Fanny Gray* was pirated back to England a year after its American publication in a slightly altered version, the spelling changed to Grey.

By the 1850s a New York publisher, Clark, Austin & Smith, printed paper dolls called Miss Florence, Miss Hattie, and other popular names of the period, and sold them in pretty little envelopes. These were, of course, cheaper than the elaborate boxed sets, and proved very popular. Brown, Taggard & Chase also offered Chandler designs in paper packages, handsomely lithographed and decorated, including Little Fairy Lightfoot and May Queen. Anson Randolph and Peter Thomson, other early American paper-doll printers, each used an easily recognizable style of illustration. These dolls were eagerly received by American children, and many found their way back to England and the Continent to be copied.

The 1840s saw the rise in popularity of the illustrated book. The art of steel engraving had reached a high point in the early 1800s, but artists revived interest in woodcuts. By the middle of the nineteenth century, the woodcuts were the favorite method of reproducing pictures.

New magazines helped to make woodcuts popular. *Punch* appeared in 1841, *The Illustrated London News* in 1842. Munich had a weekly paper called the *Fliegende Blatter*, *The New York Herald,* started in 1834, began using woodcuts a few years later. These publications featured illustration indelibly wedded to text and did much to further interest in the work of such artists as George Cruikshank, Sir John Tenniel, and Kate Greenaway, who were among the first great book illustrators.

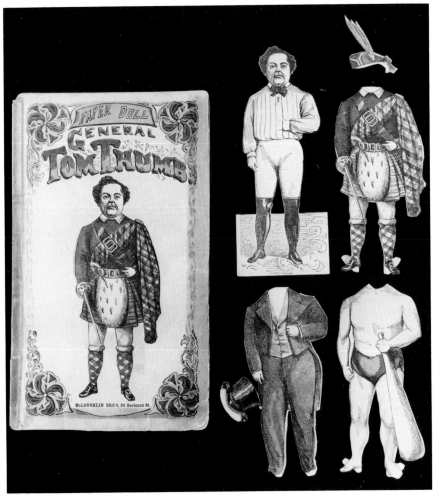

Susie, a paper doll from the series "Susie's Pets," McLoughlin Brothers, New York, c. 1859. Such hand-colored dolls (often painted by child laborers) influenced Sir John Tenniel's illustrations for *Alice in Wonderland.*

One of the first celebrity paper dolls was this McLoughlin version of "General" Tom Thumb, P. T. Barnum's famous midget star; c. 1864.

Respect for children was gaining ground; in 1847 the British Factory Act restricted the working day for children to ten(!) hours.

Illustrated books—and the beginnings of reform of conditions for children—influenced paper playthings. Conventions for paper dolls were established: dolls became full figures wearing underclothing, not just the movable heads of the Fuller period. Doll and clothing were printed flat, and were seldom precut by the manufacturer; rather, they were sold in the cheaper form to be cut at home. Folders or envelopes took the place of boxes.

The first company to profit enormously from mass-market paper toys was McLoughlin Brothers, New York. McLoughlin designs established the pattern of paper dolls for years to come. The little leaflets folded into inexpensive envelopes were printed in several sizes sold at different prices. The most popular editions were larger than those of all the other manufacturers.

By 1850, with printing both better and cheaper, McLoughlin had begun printing paper soldiers, children's books, and doll houses complete with paper furniture and people. Their earliest paper dolls came out just before the Civil War. They were hand colored, since labor cost less than color reproduction by machine. Much of that labor was done

by children, whose small fingers were deemed suitable for the tricky coloring work. Because of the hand coloring, each McLoughlin doll of this period is different.

McLoughlin dolls had a special look; prim, serious, expressive faces set on stiff bodies. The style seems familiar today because Tenniel, in his celebrated illustrations for *Alice in Wonderland,* showed an awareness of the look of McLoughlin dolls, knowing that they would fit the popular conception of little girls of the day. Many McLoughlins were produced between 1854 and 1911, when the company went out of business. Their catalogs show a fascinating collection of games, books,

alphabets, and all kinds of inexpensive paper toys.

McLoughlin dolls usually came in three sizes, selling for a penny, a nickel, and fifteen cents. Two of the very earliest were of Topsey (spelled with an *e*) and Little Eva St. Clair, characters in Harriet Beecher Stowe's bestseller, *Uncle Tom's Cabin*. Topsey and Eva were the first paper dolls known to be inspired by a popular novel. Topsey is also the first known black paper doll.

History showed up in McLoughlin designs, as well. General and Mrs. Tom Thumb, the midgets made famous by P.T. Barnum, were popular enough to have been issued in elaborate back-and-front versions with costumes beautifully detailed and colored. A later doll was based on the baby produced, according to Barnum, by the famous couple.

McLoughlin dolls show characteristic design similarities. These little dolls sometimes pop up in the pages of old magazines, in cigar boxes, inside children's books, or even as junk sold at antique shows

and flea markets. Since they were the first mass-market paper dolls in America, there are many still to be found. And since they were considered precious playthings—their fifteen-cent price was worth more in the nineteenth century than it is now—they were carefully preserved by their owners. Several collectors specialized in McLoughlins.

By the middle of the nineteenth century, America had fashion magazines for women, like the ones which had appeared a few years earlier in England. One of the most popular was *Godey's Lady's Book*. This showed patterns, fashions, and household goods, and surrounded them with light fiction and household hints for women.

Magazines flourish when they really understand the needs of the readers. In 1859 Godey added two paper-doll pages to his magazine, showing four girls and two boys on one sheet and their cutout clothes on the second. Godey believed that a woman could better absorb his magazine if it contained a page or two to help quiet the children. If the page could also sell patterns, so

much the better. He was somewhat ahead of his time, it seems, because the idea was not repeated. Godey anticipated by sixty years, the millions of magazine paper-doll pages—the Lettie Lanes, Betty Bonnets, and Betsy McCalls—that amused children while their mothers read in peace.

Conventions soon developed for the paper-doll sheet. The serial was designed to encourage children to buy more than one doll and to collect them. Pictures of cousins, servants, and animals spurred the child's wish for more. The idea of using celebrities as models was established, so that paper dolls reflected contemporary interests and pastimes. Children accepted paper as a substitute for costly wooden and tin toys, bisque, and china dolls.

The first hundred years set patterns for almost every paper-doll design that followed. Paper dolls were becoming big business, employing artists and printers by the hundreds, as they captured the interests of more children every year.

McLoughlin paper dolls are favorites among collectors, and although all share design characteristics, each has its own individual flavor. Typical McLoughlins include Little Pet, a well-dressed young girl, c. 1865; Susan Lee, a demure young woman of fashion, c. 1860; Dame Trot, a picturesque matron, c. 1870; the Marquis, an elegant male aristocrat, c. 1870; and most popular, Maud, the prim child, c. 1870.

3

Victorian, Edwardian, and Turn-of-the-Century Paper Dolls

By the 1880s, paper dolls were selling out in toy stores and bookshops in America, England, and the European capitals. Small scissors had become inexpensive enough for a middle-class child to own. The prices of paper dolls were such that all but the poorest child could affort them. As substitutes for expensive toys, paper toys seemed a great value to middle-class parents.

Little girls were still taught to sew, and their patience and small-muscle practice were happily transferred to paper-doll play. Children had begun to add designs of their own to the wardrobes that came with their favorite figures. They seized on fancy papers and scraps from their mothers' sewing baskets to make the pretty extra dresses that are such a pleasure to find today. Many of these little home-made dolls, some of them with dresses carefully fashioned from gold lace and trim, are in antique shops.

Less talented little girls made their own paper dolls by cutting out magazine pictures of beauti-fully dressed men, women, and children. Often they wrote names for these families on the backs of their cutouts. Some children created scrapbooks of houses and rooms filled with paper furniture and people cut from current magazines. Most children had the skills, materials, and leisure time for paper play, and manufacturers increased their output every year.

Magazines and newspapers began featuring paper dolls regularly. Some of these dolls were elaborate and beautiful. With so many paper-doll designs needed for publication, the search for ideas was on. Subjects branched out from the pictures of women and children's fashions toward anything that might interest or educate a child. The need was for subjects that offered groupings or collections, such as Mother Goose characters or the kings and queens of England, thereby encouraging a child to gather the whole series. The family was a popular subject, since children identified with families, and families could be extended. Each publication could produce its own family, as *McCall's* magazine produced Betsy's in a later era.

Dozens of serial subjects began to appear. Heroes and heroines of American history came out as paper dolls in the United States. Royal paper dolls appeared in England, Germany, and Austria. There were serial paper dolls showing historical costume, soldiers' uniforms, occupations, Shakespeare's characters, and many more subjects. One American magazine issued paper dolls based on children in famous art masterpieces. Germany produced beautiful folders with groups of paper sheets of royal and aristocratic families. Paper dolls were designed for royal weddings, and to commemorate such occasions as Victoria's jubilee. Royal paper dolls, embossed and printed in several rich colors, faithfully portrayed celebrities and their wardrobes.

In the 1880s, ladies in parlors made scrapbooks, screens, boxes, and fans with scraps of paper, an art called decoupage. They used lit-

Girls frequently made their own paper dolls by cutting out pictures from fashion magazines. These four homemade dolls show stylish American costumes; c. 1885.

A folder containing *Ankleidepuppen* "in the latest fashion," Germany, c. 1845. The folders were often as attractive as their contents.

An *Ankleidepuppen* sheet with three lovely paper girls, Amanda, Fernande, and Kathy; Germany, c. 1845.

tle embossed pictures sold in sheets often connected by little tabs. These were carefully separated and pasted down, sometimes in designs, and then lacquered over. Many of the trays, screens, and boxes are prized antiques today. Paper dolls were a children's version of this pastime. Often the subject matter for scrapbooks and screens was the same as for children's play.

What McLoughlin was to America, a toy maker named Raphael Tuck was to England. Tuck published large, costly paper dolls, toys, books, and games. Expensive sets of all the English sovereigns, of animals, soldiers, grotesque figures, and English landscape scenes were issued year after year. Many were lovely enough to be used by women for decoupages, and have been preserved by the coat of lacquer. Others were pasted into scrapbooks kept in Victorian parlors to be enjoyed over and over.

Fortunately for collectors, Tuck made a practice of labeling and dating many of its printed products. The backs of the paper dolls and

their clothing are all clearly marked, making it easy to know when a set is complete.

The firm of Raphael Tuck & Sons Ltd. was established in London in 1866 by a German immigrant

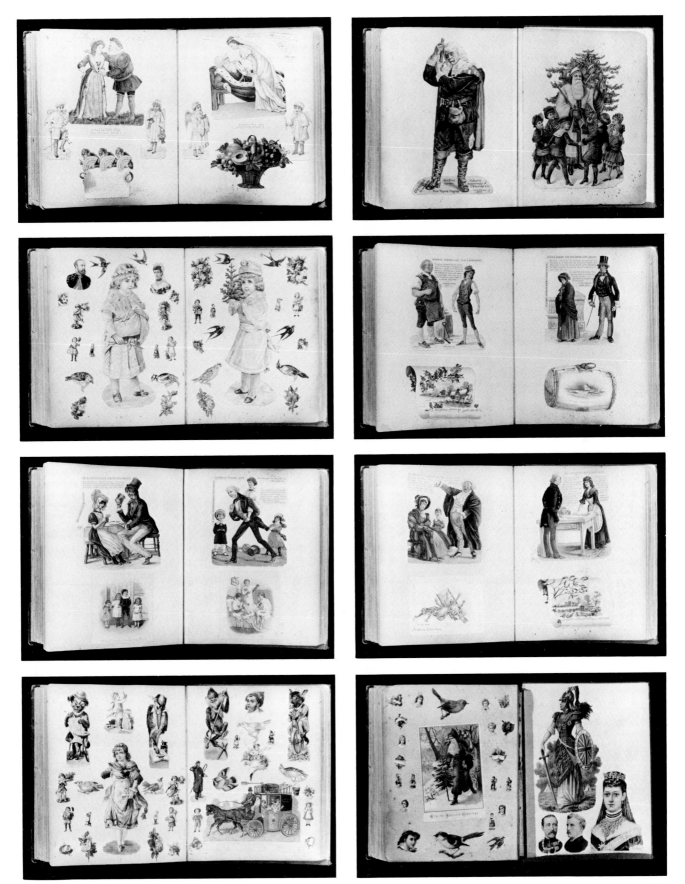

printer. It was first a fine-art print business, producing the oleographs and chromolithographs that the Germans had developed. An ambitious man with a hard-working family, Tuck rapidly expanded his business to include postcards, book-plates, picture stamps, scenic and animal pictures. In 1871 he produced elegant Christmas cards, encouraging public interest in them with design contests. The Tuck "Chromo Portrait Gallery" of the royal family was enormously popular. With aggressive merchandising and an instinct for public taste, Tuck had established a trademark, and had been granted a royal warrant of appointment to Queen Victoria. The popularity of Tuck work grew quickly in England and soon spread to other countries. The firm, expanded and changed, exists to this day, although during the 1940 London blitz a German bomb destroyed all the early plates and designs. To Tuck goes the credit for encouraging the vast industries which grew to sell valentines, postcards, greeting cards, and scrap.

While all paper dolls are based on subjects that reflect the interests of contemporary women and girls, no subject has proved as lasting as the wedding. When Tucks were produced, marriage was the goal of

Paper dolls inspired some extraordinary homemade collages, among which is this scrapbook, dated Christmas 1890, made by a Parisian mother for her child. Among the Christmas cards, bits of music, and miscellaneous paper figures are paper-doll treasures from Raphael Tuck and Sons, London. They include figures representing British sovereigns, battle scenes, characters from literature (Shakespeare, Bunyan, and Dickens), as well as Britannia, symbol of Great Britain (*preceding page*).

Belle of Newport is an elegant Tuck doll with characteristically sweet face and elaborate outfits, including contemporary tennis gown; 1894.

every little girl, and weddings were as large and lavish as a family's finances would allow. This single great moment in a woman's life was regarded as an ideal paper-doll subject, allowing for relatives, friends, clergy, servants, and others to surround the happy pair. Wedding paper dolls appear in every period of paper-doll history, but few are lovelier than the early Tuck examples.

The Tuck adult dolls have a distinctive look, and so did Tuck children, which were usually named by the manufacturer and marked on the figure. Winsome Winnie, Sweet Alice, and Merry Marion record popular Victorian girls' names, as Lordly Lionel and Royal Regie are recorded by Tuck for boys' names. From this time on, paper dolls with names reflect popular taste; Victorian favorites such as Abigail, Harriet, and Beatrice would give way to movie star's names, but in the 1890s Dolly, Gladys, and Dottie were to the popular mode. Tuck dolls came often in several sizes, like the McLoughlins.

Always alert for subjects that could be serialized, Tuck established

the traditions of paper dolls, with costumes from foreign lands, fairy-tale costumes, English regional clothing, and so forth. One 1894 series featured stage celebrities Ada Rehan, Julia Marlowe, Maude Adams, and Mrs. Leslie Carter, with costumes from their various theatrical successes.

Clothing for Tuck dolls slipped on beneath the chin, a style which did not catch on with other manufacturers. It probably worked well for the expensive Tucks which were made of pasteboard, but flimsier dolls would have been quickly destroyed by this method of attaching paper clothes. Other makers were beginning to use the little tabs that we associate with paper dolls, or else to use the back-and-front clothing for two-sided dolls, a favorite of McLoughlin.

Tuck dolls are fairly easy to find

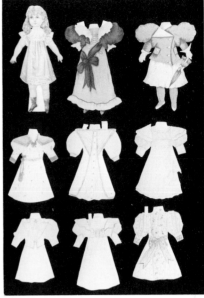

The Bridegroom is from an outstanding Tuck wedding set, 1894. Like the Belle, this doll is cardboard, 9½ inches high, precut, and very smartly garbed.

at antique shows and fairs, especially if you are willing to be patient about assembling the sets, since hats and dresses are often found mixed in with other paper memorabilia. The markings on the backs make them easy to identify and group. A complete set of Tuck dolls with its folder, in good condition, costs well over $100 today. The more elaborate sets come to a great deal more, since they contain several dolls with costumes and headgear.

Nothing makes the importance of hats clearer than collecting nineteenth-century paper dolls. All the people had hats to match their costumes as a matter of course. At this period no lady would go out of doors, even to her own garden, without covering her head, and even workmen wore caps. Finding the proper hat for each costume is a paper-doll challenge. The Tuck hats

are labeled like the dresses, so that this group is simpler for beginners. Learning to note the exact color of a dress, the texture of the paper, and the condition of the back of the paper comes later. Patience and search will help assemble many Tuck sets for far less money than buying complete matched sets.

The success of Tuck designs were copied everywhere. Many advertisers borrowed the look and style of Tuck children. Manufacturers in other countries borrowed the form, placing cardboard dolls in matched sets into folders like the Tuck envelopes.

Just as the women's magazines were eyeing the success of the Tuck dolls and putting paper dolls into their own pages, so were American newspapers. The ideal paper-doll vehicle was the Sunday supplement, printed on heavy paper and able to hold beautiful color and detailed design. Since these were weeklies, the need for design ideas was greatly stepped up.

The most famous of all Sunday supplement dolls of this period was a group called the Boston *Herald*

Dolly Delight, a well-named Tuck doll of 1902. The six extra dresses were handmade.

Tuck dolls inspired many imitations, including Prinzessin Tausendschön ("Princess Thousand Beauties"), Germany, c. 1890.

Ladies. These were produced in 1895 and 1896 as a fashion series, and were immensely popular with women and little girls. The large figures, a blonde and a brunette on cardboard sheets 10½ inches high were offered by mail. Dressed in corsets and petticoats, their faces suggest the Charles Dana Gibson drawings which were a feminine ideal of the period.

Every Sunday for two years, the *Herald* published costumes for these dolls to wear interchangeably. The uncut sheets show that a back view of each costume was included, suggesting that women used these dolls as guides for home dressmaking. The kinds of clothes pictured tell us a great deal about the dreams and fancies of women at this time. Yachting clothes, opera toilettes, and tea gowns may not have been the everyday wear of women who read 1895 newspapers, but they were the sort of clothes women read about in novels by Henry James (and others less gifted) and seen on wealthy ladies who set styles. The Boston *Herald* Ladies served the same function as today's glossy high-fashion magazines; allowing women a careful look at the clothes of the rich.

A few of the original plates for these illustrations have been found, bearing only the name of the lithographers. These plates were evidently sold to many newspapers to be published under their own banners, since *Herald* Ladies turn up from newspapers printed all over America. You can find these sheets, or cut copies of the costumes, in many antique shops, if you can identify them. Finding the dolls can be more difficult, but they turn up, too. Several have been found framed and dressed in fabric costumes, since the figures are large, sturdy, and inspiring for amateur designers.

In 1895 the Boston *Globe,* evidently in response to the popularity of the *Herald* paper dolls, began is-

Sunday supplements proved ideal vehicles for fashion paper dolls. One of the most famous series was issued by the Boston *Herald*. This Boston *Herald* Lady, 10½ inches high, is a fine example; 1895.

Herald Ladies in three fashionable outfits: wedding gown (1895), swimsuit (1895), and opera cloak (1896).

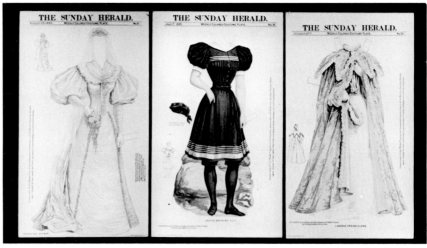

Other newspapers followed the *Herald's* lead in offering paper dolls in their Sunday supplements. This version of champion bicyclist Albert Zimmerman appealed to boys; Boston *Globe*, 1895.

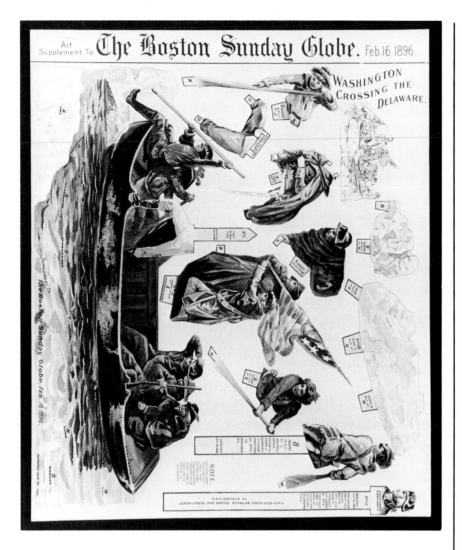

Hours of fun awaited the child who cut out and assembled this patriotic tableau of Washington crossing the Delaware (complete with ice floes); Boston *Globe,* 1896.

suing what they called art supplements. These covered a vast range of subjects, since the designs needed were so numerous. Wedding parties, fashion dolls, soldiers and sailors, nursery-rhyme figures, holiday scenes, occupations, historical scenes and places, and celebrities came pouring forth. These dolls were meant to be cut and assembled, on the theory that they gave a child more work than simply cutting out clothing, and would thus be of greater interest. This did not prove true; the results were less than satisfactory because the scenes did not stay assembled. Transparent adhesive tape had not been invented, and the tabs provided to make the toys work were often destroyed in the cutting.

These full-color supplements were printed without names and sold to various papers, the *Globe* being the largest distributor. Such lithographers as Forbes, Ottmann, American Lithographers, Joseph P. Schiller, and Edwards, Deutsch & Heitmann were among the designers and producers. Often these paper dolls are referred to collectively as Forbes dolls.

Educational subjects echoed the Tuck designs. American history was used, but European history was included, too. All the designs reflect the interests of the society that enjoyed them. The patriotic sentiment which reached a high point in the 1890s shows over and over in these scenes; even the Spanish-American War of 1898 provided subject matter about the people of the Philippines in paper-doll form.

The stage and opera stars who were the celebrities Americans knew best were often featured as paper dolls. What yesterday's children had to learn from newspapers, today's learn from their television screens. But in turn-of-the-century America, paper dolls taught children about a world wider than their own home towns. Many first learned about foreign lands from paper dolls that showed native costumes and flags of the nations. Tuck had printed a series called "Children of Many Lands," sold both in die-cut and flat-sheet form. This was copied in America by McLoughlin in a set called "The New Model Book of Dolls," which was later reprinted with changes as "Wide World Costume Dolls." Magazines, newspapers, and product advertisers kept an eye on what was selling in the toyshops to inspire their designs. Children of foreign lands remained a paper-doll subject of interest for many years to come, widening the eyes of land-bound American children before travel was possible for any but the wealthy.

With the success of newspaper and magazine paper dolls, American advertisers issued a great body of material of their own. America was still in an era when only the rich spent large sums on children's toys from shops. Most toys were made

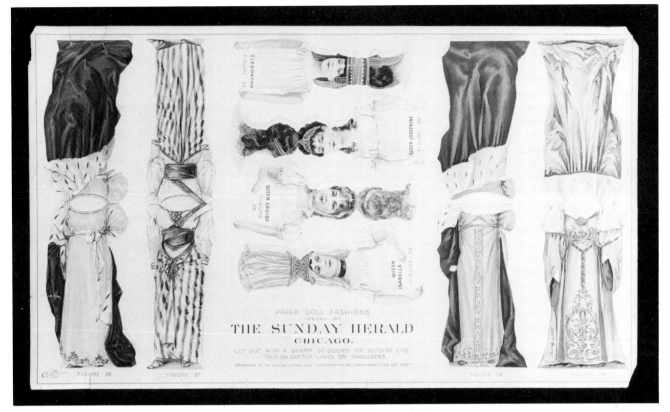

Royalty fascinated democratic America, as seen in this Chicago *Herald* paper-doll page featuring four famous queens—Cleopatra, Josephine, Marie Louise, and Isabella—and their period costumes; 1895.

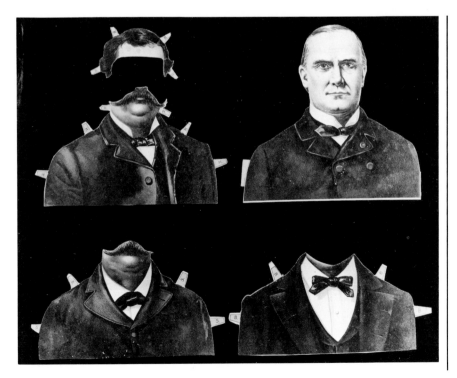

An unusual paper-doll montage of the leading contenders in the 1896 American presidential elections, William Jennings Bryan and William McKinley; c. 1896.

at home, at little or no cost. Paper dolls cut from newspapers or magazines, or issued by manufacturers for pennies, were available to nearly all children. Product makers jumped on this bandwagon to get children collecting paper-doll sets and to keep asking their parents to buy brands by name. This merchandising practice still prevails in America.

Paper dolls were particularly suited for use in and on product packaging. They were printed on wrap-

An early example of paper dolls used for advertising, this winsome trio declares "Our Mammas use Pearline" soap; c. 1895.

Flower-girl paper dolls make charming advertisements; U.S., c. 1895.

pers, cereal boxes, and package labels, as well as inserted into coffee bags, flour packages, sugar and tobacco sacks. When a product's packaging could not actually accommodate the paper doll, mail orders were advertised on the packages, so that the dolls could be sent for with a proof of purchase and a few pennies.

Paper dolls were ideal for sending through the mails, and advertisers quickly adopted the idea. They often copied or adapted designs from the European embossed paper dolls which were so popular in the toyshops.

The artwork of advertising paper dolls was charming, the colors bright, and the look unmistakable for its period. But most designs were stolen back and forth, used for several companies, and often featured families, nursery-rhyme characters, foreign costumes, adult occupations, and other serial subjects.

All advertising dolls, of course, had printed messages, which makes identification easy for novices. They are a study in themselves, rich in ad-

jectives and claims that the Federal Trade Commission would frown upon, particularly for the "nerve cures" and tonics of the period, which claimed to cure every known disease.

Advertising dolls still exist. Such giant companies as the Ford Motor Company, Lever Brothers, and Colgate used paper dolls in the 1940s to advertise their products. Eiderlon, a lingerie maker, used paper dolls to advertise bikini underwear in 1979 and 1980. And no less sophisticated an advertiser than Bloomingdale's in New York ran newspaper ads with paper dolls in 1979. See the section on advertising paper dolls in Part Two of this book.

Paper houses were popular in the early 1900s. This idealized public school was issued by McLoughlin in 1901.

Dancing paper dolls, direct descendants of the *pantin,* imported to the U.S. from the German firm Littauer and Bauer, 1895. The black baby and the adult dancer were favorites.

Model villages and houses were popular at the turn of the century, and even more popular was the activated paper doll, a direct descendant of the first *pantins.* The company best known for selling these dancing dolls in America was the Dennison Manufacturing Company. The dolls were large, from 9 to 14 inches high, with heads, arms, and legs made of stiff, glossy pasteboard. They were sold in envelopes as parts of sets with tissue and crepe paper in many colors meant for costuming the dolls at home, and with directions, for what this modest age called "body forms." The dolls came in different styles, from babies to dancers, and the sets held ornamental gilt papers, lace papers,

stars, and more. A popular subject for dolls like the Dennisons was a black baby, sometimes with a wide grin. By 1905, the Dennison catalog offered nine designs, including ballerinas in three sizes at five, eight, and ten cents apiece, and primadonnas, 16½ inches high, for fifteen cents.

Collectors agree that while many of these dolls were assembled in New York, the lithographed heads and parts were made by a German firm called Littauer & Bauer, which operated from about 1880 until Hitler shut down the company in the 1930s. Many of the activated dolls carry an L&B monogram and a patent mark. Some had faces vaguely based on famous actresses of the

Happy and sad baby heads were lithographed in Germany and exported to the U.S.; Littauer and Bauer, c. 1895. Their distinctly European faces add to their charm.

Dancing doll dressed in homemade tissue clothes, U.S., c. 1895. Long hours and great patience were needed to form the ruffles and pleats.

Hortense, an embossed paper doll whose elegant wardrobe is impressively ornate and detailed; U.S., c. 1885.

work into tiny ruchings and pleats of tissue paper. The rosettes and ruffles were quite as elegant and ornate as the costumes of the period. Women and children who worked long hours making fancy clothes for flat dolls also designed dolls and costumes from scratch. The turn of the century was the start of the great age of homemade dolls.

day, like Della Fox and Ada Rehan. These activated dolls were often beautifully dressed by ladies and older children and framed for parlors. They even appeared on the bureaus of bachelors, as early pin-up girls, in a period before photographs of stars were available.

Sometimes you find sheets of these dolls in stores which specialize in old paper, valentines, and postcards. They are also found put together with staples in antique shops. Less fragile than most paper dolls, this group is better preserved and easier to handle. Even more interesting are the tissue clothes you can sometimes find; complete with hats, they tell a great deal about the restricted lives of upper-class women of the time, who poured creative

England's Tucks were activated at this time, too. A doll called Daisy Dimple inaugurated a set of little clowns, Chinese and Japanese figures, each with its own tiny toys. One is a Pierrot in the old *pantin* tradition. These dolls were hinged at the shoulders and moved by a cord at the back, just as the first *pantin* had been strung to make them dance. By the beginning of the twentieth century, paper dolls were borrowing ideas from earlier forms and using new techniques based on older ones.

The popular taste for beauty when the century turned was set by Gibson drawings, Broadway star Lillian Russell, and London's Flora-dora Girls. England's Princess (later Queen) Alexandra, expensively and beautifully fashion conscious, set a standard for the dress of the wealthy. Her wardrobe was famous far beyond her country's borders, and her figure as a paper doll, embossed and gilded, is one of the most beautiful of all dolls.

The world of children's books was coming under the influence of the land of Oz, the first tale in that famous series having been published in 1900. Booth Tarkington and Rudyard Kipling stories appeared in illustrated editions, making pictures in print familiar and meaningful to a generation of children. Products of all kinds had labels on which care and design excellence had been lavished. Even the lowly cigar label was beautifully printed, gilded, and embossed. These all influenced paper-doll design.

But probably the most important event of the period for paper dolls was the opening by F. W. Woolworth of the first of his stores with the familar red-and-gold fronts. Fifty-nine stores carried the signs. For the next fifty years American girls would make some of their most momentous decisions about which paper-doll book to buy next with their pennies.

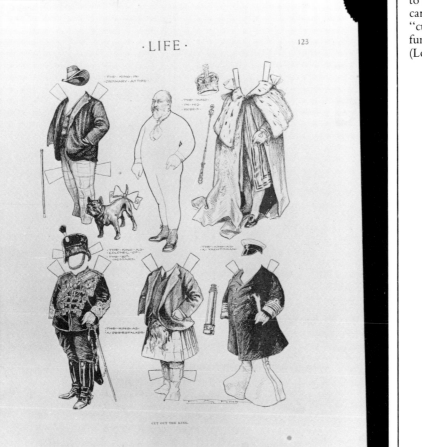

The paper-doll motif was discovered to have intrinsic humor. This caricature of Edward VII is labeled "cut out the king," and pokes gentle fun at the monarch. *Life* Magazine (London), 1901.

4
The Age of Innocence

By 1900 there existed a group of books written specifically for children in which the pictures were as memorable as the words. The Tenniel drawings for Lewis Carroll's *Alice in Wonderland,* Edward Lear's own pictures for his nonsense books, Kipling's illustrations for the *Just So Stories,* and Cruikshank's engravings for Grimm are all examples, and there are many more. Reginald Birch's illustrations for *Little Lord Fauntleroy* by Frances Hodgson Burnett influenced the dress of thousands of little boys after the book was published in 1886.

Authors of first quality delighted in writing for children, and illustrators of first quality soon joined them. Beatrix Potter, Kate Greenaway, and Randolph Caldecott executed beautiful pictures especially for children. More and more people shared the attitude that children were a special group, glorified by William Blake and William Wordsworth, entitled to art and literature of their own.

For the first time in history the children's magazine was possible. In America there was the *Youth's Companion,* for which Kipling, Tennyson, Gladstone, Wells, and Longfellow wrote, as did many other great names in literature. *St. Nicholas,* lavishly illustrated, was edited by Mary Mapes Dodge, whose own *Hans Brinker* had been illustrated by no less an artist than Thomas Nast.

The great American paper-doll publishers began printing booklets and sheets of beautiful drawings. In 1900 Arthur Saalfield bought out the publishing department of a printing company in Akron, Ohio. He began to produce fine children's books to be sold through the new chain stores springing up all over America. This publishing effort gradually led to coloring books, painting books, and paper-doll books enjoyed by millions of children.

Western Publishing Company started in 1907 as a basement print shop with two battered presses. Its Whitman subsidiary was begun in 1915. Whitman went on to publish millions of games, activity books, and paper dolls for children.

The new standards of graphics for children was high. The book business had taught publishers how much money there was in good art for children. This influenced the paper-doll designers and the businessmen who planned the publishing efforts.

In England the production of embossed paper dolls of royalty flourished. Almost all the immediate members of Victoria's large family, and the people they married, were popular paper figures. Their elaborate design, faithful portraiture, and expensive paper show the attention given to paper dolls; an earlier age would not have bothered with anything like them for a child, nor would these dolls have been available at a reasonable price even fifty years later. But after the turn of the century, graphic skills and technical abilities made these paper figures appropriate for children with the leisure to enjoy them and the willingness to care for them.

Handmade dolls were always an alternative for creative, as well as for poor, children. These are from a large and expressive set with individualized faces; Philadelphia, c. 1904.

The Lettie Lane paper family, one of the best-loved magazine paper-doll series, was introduced by this page in the *Ladies' Home Journal*, 1908. Sheila Young's creations were consistently imaginative and interesting, with a pastel pretty look. (*Ladies' Home Journal*).

Children were making their own paper dolls, or prevailing on talented adult amateur artists to design for them. In a period when watercolor techniques were part of the general education of a lady, it was natural to create litte watercolor paper dolls at home.

Sets of these dolls, found in antique shops from time to time, tell us that making paper dolls was a home pastime. Women barred from working outside the home, and sick children, found distraction in work like this, and the results were recognized as precious enough to preserve. Some sets seem as fresh as they must have looked when they were painted a century ago.

Not everyone was skillful enough to make drawings and paintings at home. The demand for paper dolls kept growing, and the magazines and advertisers hurried to supply it. In 1908 the *Ladies' Home Journal* introduced Lettie Lane, a paper-doll series by artist Sheila Young. It was to delight little girls almost once a month for seven years, and was immediately fol-

33

Sheila Young focused on different members of Lettie's family to increase the variety of figures and situations. From the series presenting Lettie's sister's wedding come the maid of honor, the minister and the best man, and five of the younger wedding guests; 1909–1910. (*Ladies' Home Journal*).

Lettie gave an "around-the-world party" to give Young the chance to draw exotic people and costumes, including a Chinese boy and girl, a Norwegian boy, girl, and nurse, and a French girl with dolls and puppets of her own; 1910–1911. (*Ladies' Home Journal*).

lowed by a similar series of the same size, Betty Bonnet, which lasted until 1918. The whole forms the most detailed record possible of family clothes, possessions, and activities, all seen from a child's viewpoint.

Once Lettie's immediate family was introduced with suitable clothing and accessories, the artist featured other family members in memorable ways. Young was ingenious in devising ways to keep the series fresh; for example, she showed Lettie's grandparents as adults and as the children they had been, allowing her to use costumes from an earlier time. A child could save each successive page and possess an enormous group of paper figures to use in imaginative play. Judging from the names often found penciled on the backs of cut Lettie Lanes, children used them to make up families of their own. Today the most progressive toy makers offer wooden and plastic doll families to stimulate children's emotions and imaginations; yesterday's children used Sheila Young's drawings for the same purposes.

Lettie was given a twin brother and sister, carrying on a theme which has always been popular in the world of paper dolls. Later there were triplet paper dolls for children, and of course the Dionnes inspired quintuplets of all kinds at a still later time.

The wedding played a key part in the family series; Lettie's older sister appeared as a bride in a series complete with a minister and best man. The wedding lasted more than eight issues and provided a focal point for grouping all the dolls in their best clothes. The next stage was, the honeymoon. This carried the designs into the fresh territory of foreign lands. Lettie's sister traveled all over Europe, as well as in China and Japan, so that Young could refresh the series with native costumes.

Young understood the natural affinity between paper dolls and real dolls. Most children who loved dolls gravitated to paper dolls, too. Although flat and flimsy by comparison, the paper ones offered a chance for a far larger number of dolls, and a collection that could be stored in a small place. It was easy to add clothes and people to paper, even for an untrained artist. With the Lettie Lane paper dolls, the number of American children who collected dolls in shoe boxes, cigar boxes, folders, and notebooks, and carried them to friends' houses to share, grew tremendously. Women now in their seventies and eighties who played with these dolls as children remember them in astonishing detail. Detail is part of the special intimacy of paper-doll memories. When a child has cut out and handled a paper figure, dressed it over and over, drawn extra clothing for it and carefully put that doll away over and over, the memory remains sharp.

Lettie Lane's Most Beautiful Doll as a Bride
The Doll That Has Come to Life for Every Little Journal Girl
By Sheila Young

The extras in all Sheila Young paper dolls are fascinating. There were a great many dolls within dolls, tiny figures which were adored by little girls, and which still command special prices among collectors today. The accessories for all the figures tell

Even paper dolls had dolls in Young's series. Lettie's most beautiful doll, Daisy, was available in bisque for $4.50 and three new subscriptions. Patterns for the doll's outfits, including this bridal gown, were included in the offer; 1911. (*Ladies' Home Journal*).

start all over again with fathers and mothers dressed in newer fashions, continued through World War I, and wound up with another big wedding in 1918.

This series, too, faithfully recorded popular taste. Betty's brother wears clothes which combine the look of Fauntleroy for dress and Penrod for play, which defined a boy's wardrobe in 1915. The bridegroom in the Bonnet series is, of course, an American soldier, complete with medicine kit and a handknit khaki sweater. The grownup cousins have a banjo and a chafing dish, reflecting popular rages of the day. The servants in the series, consisting of chauffeurs, chefs, and footmen as well as nurses and maids, engaged in their own war effort. The cook holds a meatless cookbook, nurse knits for the Red Cross, and the chic French maid knits for the navy, according to the book of directions she holds.

While the *Ladies' Home Journal* was boosting circulation with these paper dolls, other magazines were running their own pages for their readers' children. The *Delineator* began in 1910 with a series of "cut and paste" pictures by Lou Eleanor Colby. In 1912 Carolyn Chester invented a different sort of paper doll, called the full base, meant to be cut and curved into a standing figure. At first these rounded dolls were designed as the obligatory family; in this case, the family of Adele. But in 1913 a new series commemorated the fiftieth anniversary of Butterick Patterns, first cut in 1863 in Sterling, Massachusetts. This series featured Butterick designs throughout the years. More rounded dolls were

a great deal about the period. The bridegroom has a Kodak camera, a gun case, and laced boots. Lettie's father owns a pink hunting coat, a touch of aristocracy that gives us a notion of the wealthy American family's interest in European customs. Even the household pets in the Young series show us the breeds which were popular at the time.

In March 1915, Lettie Lane introduced another paper child and her family to *Journal* readers. Betty Bonnet, who allowed the artist to

Betty Bonnet Goes to a Wedding
The Bridegroom. By Sheila Young

Betty Bonnet's Household Servants
By Sheila Young

Sheila Young's next series was Betty Bonnet, and a whole new family of paper dolls was created. The bridegroom is from a large wartime wedding episode; note the inclusion of uniforms in the patriotic groom's wardrobe, and an early Kodak camera; 1918. (*Ladies' Home Journal*).

Betty Bonnet had an impressively large staff of household servants, including one in livery; 1918. (*Ladies' Home Journal*).

drawn by Corwin Knapp Linson in 1913, and in 1914 the magazine ran a series called "Peter Newell's Movies," a new kind of cutout that acknowledged America's new entertainment, the motion picture.

By 1916 there were many celebrity paper dolls which were drawn from movie stars, with costumes from their various roles. This tradition was to send paper-doll popularity to its height, as Hollywood grew and took over the American imagination. An early series was called "Who Are They?"; no later series would have had to ask.

McCall's, which had been published since 1876, ran an assortment

of paper dolls from 1909 on, although its family dolls never achieved the popularity of the Young work. The family included a black cook, Aunt Dinah, in the Topsey tradition of black dolls; a stereotype created by white artists. Paper-doll history is, after all, a history of clichés, a record of prevailing popular attitudes. The kind of black history recorded is the same as is found in children's books like *Little Black Sambo,* and in the valentines and greeting cards of the period. Until much later blacks in paper dolls were either servants or entertainers, much as they were in movies of the same years. Queen

Aunt Dinah, the Colored Cook, Comes to Join the Paper Doll Family

Holden, the most famous living paper-doll artist, reports designing a beautiful black baby paper doll in the 1930s which she was unable to sell. When she illustrated the *Our Gang* movie series, she was able to include a faithful, beautiful portrait of the black child. Not until the 1940s did America have black celebrity dolls as well as attractively drawn black families.

McCall's could not seem to settle on one artist, and ran many limited series dolls in the early 1900s. The magazine got its own back only in the 1950s with Betsy McCall.

A popular magazine *Pictorial Review* gave its readers the Ted E. Bear series in 1909. When a 1902 cartoon portrayed Teddy Roosevelt refusing to shoot a bear cub, the artist created the first teddy bear, and the toy world was quick to respond. Hundreds of teddy bears appeared in various materials all over the world, and collecting them is a separate branch of toy collection. The paper-doll world responded too, with a charming bear which was sold in several sizes and proved as popular as any other version. Today a reproduction of this bear is still a popular seller.

Pictorial Review introduced another long-running paper-doll heroine, Dolly Dingle. Drawn by Grace

Movie stars captured the public's fancy and soon appeared as paper dolls. Readers of the *Delineator* were asked to guess the names of these two stars, shown with four of their screen costumes; no later series would have had to ask. (Answer: William Farnum and Theda Bara, 1917). (*Butterick Fashion Marketing Company*).

McCall's magazine ran a series of paper dolls that included Aunt Dinah, the Colored Cook, 1911. Aunt Dinah unfortunately typifies the stereotyped portrayal of blacks throughout American popular culture.

Paper cutouts loosely based on Tenniel's famous illustrations for *Alice in Wonderland*, themselves influenced by paper dolls; *Pictorial Review*, 1909.

A paper-doll version of the teddy bear, still a children's favorite. J. Ottmann Lithography Company, New York, c. 1906.

Grace G. Drayton's Dolly Dingle was probably the most popular single paper doll, and certainly the cutest. Dolly has many faces and friends, including Sammy Snooks and an alluring Gracie Harriman; *Pictorial Review*, 1916, 1918, 1924.

G. Drayton, Dolly is probably the most popular single paper doll of all time. Almost two hundred pages of Dolly and her friends appeared between 1916 and 1933. She was made into a real doll, painted on china, turned into jewelry, used on stationery and many other commercial products. There is something wonderfully appealing in her plump cheeks and wicked smile, a foreshadowing of Lucy and Eloise, the model of a knowing little girl who seems to attract interest in every period. The Dolly Dingle dolls are especially familiar because the Campbell Soup Company hired Drayton to draw the Campbell Kids, the company's most popular and lasting advertising symbol. The bulk of the Dingle series appeared after World War I, but the taste was firmly established when the dolls first appeared, and reflect the innocent spirit that characterized America before the war. Drayton was particularly adept at drawing pets and accessories and in using poses that were out of the ordinary, enchanting millions of little girls and their mothers.

The Woman's Home Companion also had a famous artist working in cutout form. Rose O'Neill, who invented the Kewpie doll, presented the first of the Kewpie Kutouts in 1912. They ran in the magazine through 1914, and were taken up in many forms, just as Dolly Dingle had been. The magazine ran paper dolls for many years, although only a circus series, nursery-rhyme characters, and a wartime series appeared before the 1920s.

Good Housekeeping began a series called Little Louise in 1909. In 1919 the magazine persuaded Sheila Young to draw the Polly Pratt family of paper dolls for them, although Polly was never as beautifully drawn or printed as the artist's work for the *Journal*.

The newspapers were busy getting out paper dolls, too. The Sun-

Dolly Dingle is recognizable to millions as the prototype for the Campbell Soup Kids, also drawn by Drayton; *Pictorial Review*, c. 1922.

Good Housekeeping magazine ran Little Louise, whose friends included Rastus, 1909. No cliché is overlooked: banjo, straw hat, even a slice of watermelon. (*Good Housekeeping*).

"Polly's Paper Playmates," a syndicated series from 1911, appeared in the Baltimore *American* and the Boston *Post*. Brother Percy is shown with his West Point uniform, and Sister Prue goes to a costume ball and for an automobile ride; her outfit for the latter includes an elegant dust mask.

day supplement continued to be the most popular place for them.

Advertisers were diligent in designing paper dolls to sell products. Many products were particularly suited to this form of promotion, among them underwear; the un-

dressed figure offers a natural model.

Before the spurt of excitement over movies had taken hold, the celebrities Americans knew best were theater people. The Hearst papers issued a series in 1911 that included

Another charming supplement series, the Sunshine Family, featured back-and-front figures and costumes; Boston *American,* 1915. Note that the aptly named mother, Mrs. Patience, is twenty-six and has three children.

Interest in faraway places is a constant theme of American paper dolls. The Boston *Globe* featured a Russian girl with a huge Cossack hat in its Dolls of the Nations series, 1909.

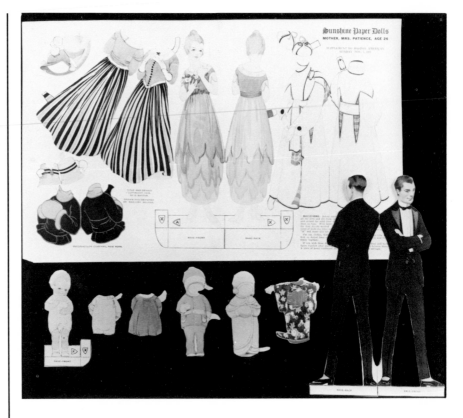

Maude Adams and opera star Geraldine Farrar.

World War I brought tremendous changes to the quality of life in America, yet the country's basic innocence is revealed in the popular wartime songs, and in paper-doll illustration. Though the *Delineator* ran a few battle scenes, artist Corwin Knapp Linson concentrated on titles like "On Leave at His Home in Sunny Italy" and "Furlough in France." Dolly Dingle joined the Red Cross, had a war garden, adopted a war orphan and held a war-savings-stamp party in various paper-doll scenes. The *Woman's Home Companion* ran paper-doll children with cute military uniforms. In general the war was reflected in paper dolls with an innocent child's view, which was not to be the case during the next war.

After 1918, people faced the realities of war. They wrote novels and painted pictures that were very different from the ones based on the

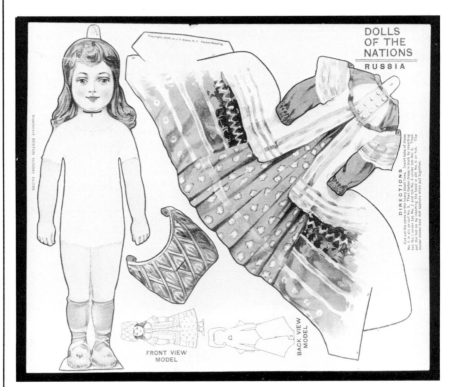

(*Facing page*)
"Boy Soldiers of All Nations," a 1905 Boston *Herald* series, included these fighting lads from India and Germany.

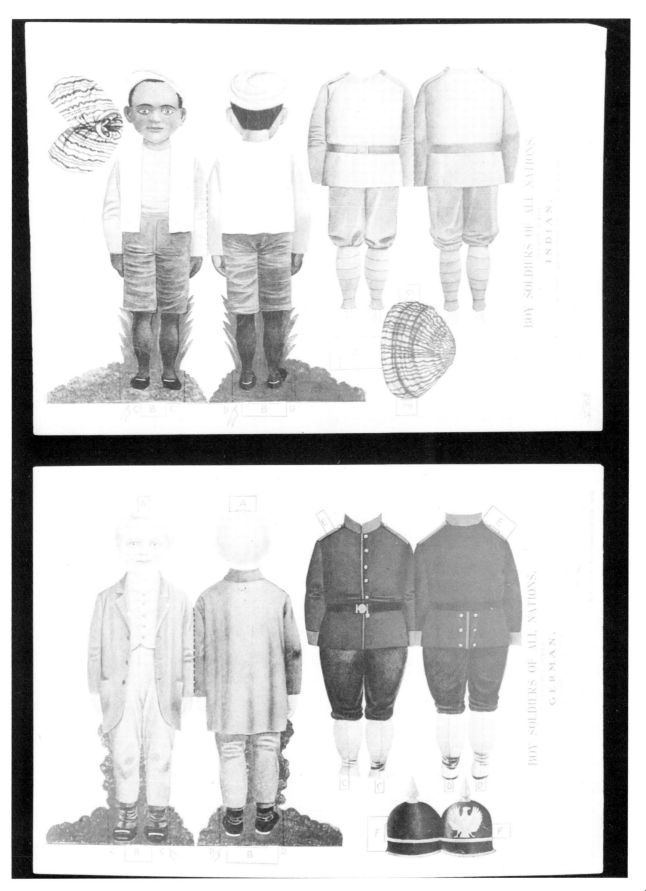

BOY SOLDIERS OF ALL NATIONS.
INDIAN.

BOY SOLDIERS OF ALL NATIONS.
GERMAN.

Miss Molly Munsing, one of the first of a number of paper dolls used, logically enough, to advertise underwear; 1909. (*Ladies' Home Journal*).

Paper-doll advertisements for the Dr. Miles Medical Company, c. 1900, took children to Russia, Sweden, Japan, and Italy.

ideals of honor, patriotism, and military glory. Before 1918, American life seemed to have order and stability; the paper-doll record of the prewar world shows large families, the progression of events in their orderly lives, their servants and possessions. Before the war, American women had not yet cut their hair short, worn cosmetics, smoked cigarettes in public, or raised their skirt hems to show any but the demure black stockings. Children were used to quiet play, and valued something as insignificant as a page from mother's magazine or father's newspaper. Radio and air travel were unknown, and most Americans stayed

close to home. Even the popular songs of the time, "Smiles" and "I'm Always Chasing Rainbows," reflected a sugary sentiment.

In 1909 artist Bertha Corbett created the Sunbonnet Babies and Overall Boys. These fat little creatures personified the faceless innocence that appealed to people before 1918. In 1910, in his *Emerald City of Oz*, L. Frank Baum and his illustrator, John R. O'Neill (Baum had fought with Denslow, who illustrated the first Oz book), paid tribute to paper dolls. Miss Cuttenclip, whose paper dolls were alive, lived in paper houses and were dressed in tissue-paper costumes, also repre-

sented an innocent world.

This world changed when the soldiers came home. One of the great influences in the postwar years was the motion picture. In its infancy at the end of the war, it taught people about a larger world and created a widely known group of celebrities with whom audiences felt on intimate terms because their faces were seen so clearly on the screen. Paper dolls based on these actors and actresses appeared immediately; Douglas Fairbanks, Mary Pickford, and Charlie Chaplin were pictured in their movie costumes. Many others, including Norma Talmadge and Mary Miles Minter, were instant fa-

ON LEAVE AT HIS HOME
IN SUNNY ITALY

Another Allied Soldier Has a Furlough

BY CORWIN KNAPP LINSON

Extra copies of this page, printed on heavy paper, without lettering on the other side, may be obtained by sending five cents postage to the Picture Editor, care of THE DELINEATOR, New York.

World War I left a paper-doll record. Corwin Knapp Linson created this set, showing "another Allied soldier [on] furlough," for the *Delineator* in 1918. Sunny Italy is at its most picturesque. (*Butterick Fashion Marketing Company*).

vorites among children, and from this time on paper dolls of movie stars were printed by the millions and collected avidly by generations of children.

It is not difficult to find paper dolls of this era for your collection. The increase in numbers of dolls produced with the large circulation of magazines and newspapers means that many still exist. You can find them in excellent condition in old magazines, sometimes still uncut.

Check any old magazine you come across for paper dolls. The prices are amazingly low, and while most of the designs are well-known and your chance of finding a unique doll slim, you can build a collection inexpensively in this way. Old cigar boxes and sewing boxes often yield cut dolls, since many little girls stored their collections this way. The prices of uncut paper dolls are usually about double the prices of cut ones. They are nearer mint con-

dition, which is the standard for paper ephemera, and they give you the advantage of knowing the set is complete. Budgetwise collectors look for cut paper dolls, which often turn up in junk piles, batches of paper memorabilia, and even in wrappings for more valuable antiques. Few dealers want to spare the time to match costumes to figures or to collect the little hats and accessories that go with each doll figure. Patience and care will save you money if you are willing to do the matching yourself. And what you learn from the look and feel of the paper is well worth your time.

The paper dolls from this period,

including celebrities, have a sweetness of expression and a style of romantic illustration that proclaims their period. The Young and Drayton dolls are unmistakable, and good identification books are available for both artists. They are a wonderful starting place for a beginner collector. The taste for sweetness and light carried over into the early 1920s and many paper-doll collectors prefer work from this period most of all.

After World War I more little girls than ever had play time, pennies, cutting skills, and interest in paper toys. They were not yet distracted by comic books, large numbers of movies, or radio and television shows. This combination of circumstances increased the manufacture and distribution of paper-dolls enormously during the following twenty years.

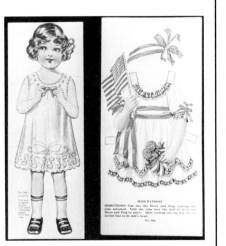

Nancy is transformed into Miss Patriot, the victorious American flag in her hand; U.S., c. 1918.

Mary Pickford, "America's Sweetheart," was a natural paper-doll heroine. The doll and the movie-based costumes are from *Photoplay,* an early fan magazine, 1919. (*The Macfadden Group, Inc.*).

Romanticism was the order of the day in the early 1900s, and the cover of "Fairy Favorite Cut Out Dolls" is no exception. M. A. Donohue, Chicago, 1913.

Lois Lenski's cover for "Dolls from
Fairy Land" is all innocent charm.
Nourse Company, New York, 1921.
(*Platt and Munk Company*).

5
The Great Years

The 1920s and 1930s in America were the greatest years of paper-doll production. Millions of little girls collected vast numbers of paper dolls, designed extra clothing for printed dolls, played with their favorites imaginatively until the dolls fell to pieces. Women who were children in those years remember their dolls thoroughly, and get special pleasure from finding them again today. Fortunate ones who lived in spacious houses with attics and basements still have their childhood collections. More often, children lost their paper dolls to trash cans as they grew up and moved away from home.

In *Kitty Foyle,* acclaimed when it was published in 1944 as a novel that truly captured women's emotions, Christopher Morley described the pattern of paper-doll play in those years. His heroine moves to a new town, plays on her front porch with her collection and immediately makes friends with the neighborhood children because of it. Her best friend grows up to be a decorator, and her success is

directly ascribed to her early interest in paper dolls and furniture. This is an accurate description of the involvement in paper play children felt in the 1920s and 1930s. Girls adored their paper dolls, learned from them, and often put their knowledge to use in adult careers.

There were more paper dolls to buy and more clothes for each of them than ever before. The celebrity dolls were the most prized. Movies were available even in small towns, so everyone knew the great stars. Movie magazines carefully described stars' wardrobes accurately and pictured movie costumes. And since movie stars, like the theater and opera stars who preceded them as subjects for celebrity dolls, were seen in changing costumes, they were perfect paper-doll subjects for publishers.

The magazines were filled with movie-star images, and the commercial publishers responded quickly. The Saalfield Publishing Company issued "Star Sets," immortalizing such early stars as

Mary Miles Minter, Betty Compson, and Fatty Arbuckle. Another series, "Hollywood Dollies," featured Reginald Denny and Douglas MacLean. Ruth McKenna in *My Sister Eileen* details the intense star worship of the period among children. As the Hollywood star system grew, with increasing sophistication in promotion and publicity, star paper dolls abounded.

In the 1930s, the St. Louis *Post-Dispatch* ran a series called "Movie Dressographs." It appeared in the Sunday paper almost each week for five years, drawn entirely by artist George Conrey. Some of the series featured stars from the St. Louis Muny Opera as well. Printed in color, the series included paper-doll figures of 252 celebrities of the day. Today they are a collector's challenge. The Milwaukee *Journal* also ran lengthy series which featured Merle Oberon, Jeanette MacDonald, Jean Harlow, Helen Hayes, and many more stars.

Both sets were extremely popular. They provide a record of early Hollywood that is valuable for film historians, fashion experts, and nostalgia buffs alike. Once America discovered celebrities, it went all out to lionize them. Movie-star paper dolls belong particularly to their own time and place, as does each kind of paper doll.

Commercial publishers had rarely used celebrity paper dolls until this time, relying on families, children, and fashion figures for their subject matter. But the enormous success of the newspaper and magazine celebrities gave commercial paper dolls a push into this new direction. The commercial celebrity sets outsold any paper-doll favorites of the past. The great paper-doll boom was on.

In the late 1920s and early 1930s, the paper-doll book with a star or group of stars on its cover and a lavish wardrobe clustered closely on its inside pages was a prized possession for almost every American girl. Woolworth's five-and-ten-cent stores rapidly filled their racks with handsome books from the Whitman Publishing Company, the Merrill Publishing Company, Saalfield Publishing Company, and smaller publishers.

The format became standardized. Usually a portrait doll of the star was centered on the book cover, which was of heavy-weight, stiff paper. The back of the cover often showed the star in one or two different poses, so that the costumes could have more variety and interest when they were cut out. The doll figures were usually perforated, and were pressed out rather than cut. This lent an element of some excitement, since it was quite easy to put a thumb right through your movie star.

Inside, numerous pages offered many glamorous costumes and accessories: shoes, gloves, fans, corsages, furs, and all the other exciting fashions items that people expected stars to wear. A little girl could spend a day or two of real work cut-

Jackie Coogan
The first cut-out in a series of paper dolls featuring movie children
Painted by JOHN RAE

ting out every piece, and real attention was needed for the tiny extras. A slip of the scissors could spoil a favorite gown. Repairs were made with white adhesive tape; you will often see it on mended hands, necks, and feet on dolls from this period.

Before World War II, children were still willing to work hard in order to play. This can be seen in other toys of the time. Building sets consisted of tiny blocks meant to be assembled in a specific order. Electric trains required the laying out of

Woman's Home Companion ran a beautifully drawn series of movie stars that included the most popular child stars, such as Jackie Coogan and the kids from *Our Gang* (see next page); 1925.

elaborate track systems. Doll houses needed arranging, papering, and cleaning. These took effort and concentration on the part of a child. Today children find it hard to believe

"Our Gang" as Paper Dolls

Fourth of the movie children cut-outs

Painted by
FRANCES TIPTON
HUNTER

Mary Kornman, the "nice" little girl

"Fattie"

Jackie Condon

"Freckles," who's the ringleader

Mary's hat

Before cutting out, paste the page to a sheet of heavy paper and press flat.

Cut around flaps and bend them back to hold the costumes in place.

This shoe belongs to Farina, above

The suit at the left is Fattie's

Jackie Condon often wears old clothes

Freckles looks pretty tough with these on

50

Queen Holden's glamorous versions of Claudette Colbert, Clara Bow, Anita Page, and Sue Carol set a trend for celebrity paper dolls, as did the stylish accuracy of their costumes. "Movie Star Paper Dolls," Whitman Publishing Company, 1931. (*Western Publishing Company, Inc.*).

that ten-cent purchase of a new paper-doll book could have fascinated a child. Nor can a modern child grasp the fascination that cutting out spangled costumes for remote and glamorous movie-star heroines held for a Depression child. And the cutting was only the beginning of the fun, the start of imaginative play for most girls of the 1920s and 1930s.

One example of a star who dazzled little girls with a new talent and a different kind of beauty was Sonja Henie. When the Norwegian figure skater reached American movies she was a natural for paper-doll designers. A New York television producer, Jeanne Harrison, vividly remembers using her mother's hand mirror as a miniature ice rink for her

paper Sonja's performances.

The inside pages of celebrity paper-doll books carried black-and-white studio shots of the star in different poses, used to fill in the gaps between clothes. These pictures were often carefully cut out and preserved with the dolls, adding to the star's glamor and to the publicity spread by the star's studio. During the Depression a dime could go far, but it could not top the play value of a paper-doll book.

Far and away the most popular star of the period for girls and their mothers was Shirley Temple. She appeared as the subject of ten paper-doll books before 1940, and in a number almost equal afterwards, as paper dolls detailed her growing up. She and many stars granted permission for "official authorized editions" filled with studio photographs and cute comments about the star's roles. The pages form a fascinating record of Hollywood's great days. Each costume is absolutely accurate. It had to be, since so many people had seen the movies and would be comparing the paper costumes to the real ones.

The language of the comments is picturesque. One caption for a Shirley Temple doll reads, "Next came *Baby Takes a Bow*, in which Shirley

danced her way into our hearts." Another says, "Shirley in the quaint peasant garb she wore as *Heidi*." Few writers today who want to communicate with children would

Norway's Sonja Henie skated her way into girls' hearts as a paper doll. This set had three figures, thirty-eight complete costumes, and numerous accessories; 1939. (*Merrill Publishing Company*).

The most popular movie star of the 1930s, Shirley Temple inspired ten paper-doll booklets during that decade, including this "authorized edition"; 1938. (*Saalfield Publishing Company*).

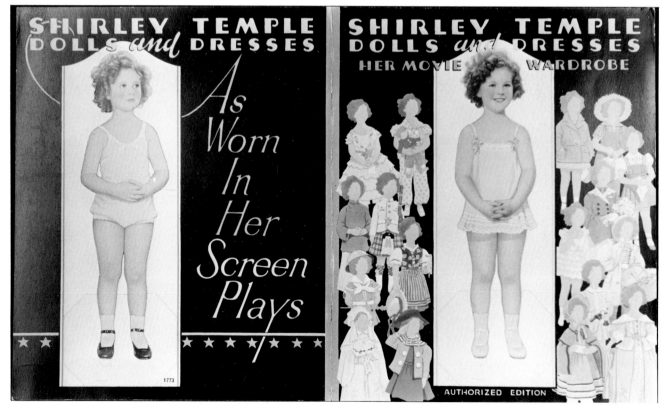

dare to use a word like *garb*.

It is rumored that Shirley Temple Black amassed millions of dollars from her share of these authorized paper-doll sets in trusts that have not yet been touched. The sets also made millions for their publishers.

Jane Withers was another popular child star and paper-doll subject, complete with her movie wardrobe. Many mothers used these books as pattern and idea books for home sewing. The clothes represent the best children's styles of the day; the fabrics so carefully illustrated are simple cottons, pure wools, and silk for party clothes. It is interesting to see that even an elaborate wardrobe for a thirties child had only one or two pairs of pants. Neat dresses, skirts, and coats were the order of the day.

The Dionne quintuplets fascinated the public in the 1930s. The quints made particularly good pa-per-doll subjects because they already formed a set. The Dionnes appeared in many versions, together and separately, and sets of anonymous quintuplets soon followed.

Advertisers also brought out paper dolls in the thirties. These were either giveaways with products or cost a few pennies less than the usual ten cents for the Woolworth's booklets. They were eagerly collected by children who had a hard time getting ten pennies together in those difficult years.

The radio, a new medium of entertainment that reached almost everyone, quickly created its own celebrities. Charlie McCarthy, the amusing wooden ventriloquist's dummy, was a favorite for children who loved his wisecrack answers to questions from Edgar Bergen. NBC radio's Mauch twins went on to movie fame in *The Prince and the Pauper*.

Although America was the leading producer of commercial paper dolls, England was still providing subjects. In 1939, Saalfield produced one of the most popular sets of all, "The Princess Paper Doll Book." This paper-doll commemorative delighted children on both sides of the Atlantic, just as its predecessors, the Victorian royal paper dolls, had done in an earlier generation. Many mothers copied the clothing in dresses for their daughters. The styles are still favorites among upper-class children in England and America.

Combining such favorite paper-doll motifs as children, family, celebrity, and royalty, Britain's princesses Elizabeth and Margaret Rose were featured as paper dolls. This set used accurate and beautiful portraits of the royal children and clothing drawn from photographs; 1939. (*Saalfield Publishing Company*).

Judging from the number of American paper-doll sets which can be found in British antique shops, a great many celebrity sets were sold in England. American movies were popular overseas, and paper-doll stars were favorites for English and European children.

The magazines of the twenties and thirties were filled with paper dolls for their readers' children. The sets cost a child nothing, since they usually were torn from a magazine already paid for, and in the Depression years anything free, however small, was a happy surprise.

The *Ladies' Home Journal,* with its history of success in the Sheila Young days, began a series based on the children's books of Lucy Fitch Perkins. While schoolchildren were reading *The Cave Twins, The Italian Twins,* and the rest of the long "Twin" series, they could cut out the characters in beautiful back-and-front versions. Pages were devoted to other fictional characters, and the ever-popular theme of children from foreign lands was brought up to date for a new generation. The magazine's thirties efforts ended with a page called "Make Your Little Girl Dresses from These Hollywood Paper Doll Cutouts," a merchandising piece which indicates the end of universal home sewing for children. The fashion industry was mass-producing children's clothing at middle-class prices.

McCall's ran paper dolls throughout the 1920s, including a fascinating set by artist Nandor Honti in art deco style. The underwear patterns in the Honti series mark the end of a long-standing tradition of home-sewn trousseaus, layettes, and household linens. For centuries, women had made these garments by hand, spending hours over their work. But by 1926, New York's Seventh Avenue was making underwear that was almost as attractive and long wearing, and that meant release from a huge sewing job.

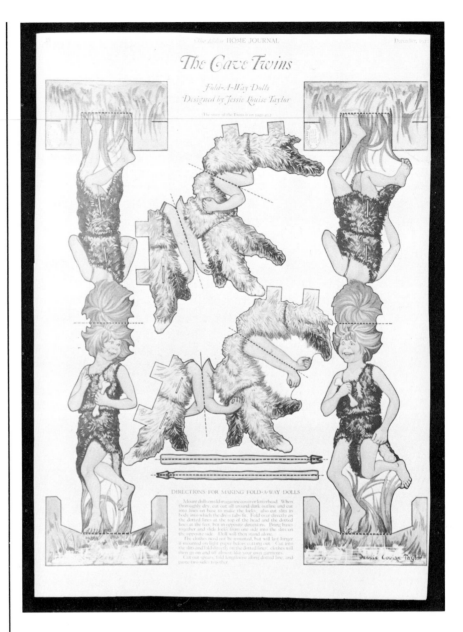

The *Ladies' Home Journal* ran paper-doll pages based on children's books, including Lucy Fitch Perkins's best-selling "Twins" series (1922) and Defoe's *Robinson Crusoe,* complete with goat, parrot, and Friday (1920). (*Ladies' Home Journal*).

The Honti paper dolls also pinpoint the art deco look that fascinated modern taste in the twenties. The 1925 Exposition Internationale des Arts Decoratifs in Paris launched a new style; the art world turned from the gentle curves and romantic look of art nouveau to the bold geometrics and strong colors of the Paris show. Because paper dolls were drawn by artists and illustrators, the new look quickly appeared in paper-doll form. The dreamy, flowery look of such artists

THE LADIES'
HOME JOURNAL

ROBINSON CRUSOE

A Page of Cut-Outs for the Children

rities did. Paper dolls reflect mass culture; high style and advanced taste have never been as popular as traditional art and close-to-home subjects. Dolly Dingle, with her cuteness and rounded curves, seemed to inspire lasting affection. While the art deco artists tried to use the latest techniques to make something new in paper dolls, little girls went on cutting out and saving the Drayton Dingles right through to 1933.

The lesson taught by Sheila Young and artists like her was that pretty children in enviable clothes sell paper dolls and avant-garde drawings do not. Even today most collectors prefer the adorable child, the cute baby and the glamorous celebrity to any paper doll that breaks artistic ground. Prices of paper dolls faithfully reflect that preference.

Artists who drew only for adults recognized the paper-doll format and often used it to get across the changing roles of a particular person. *Vanity Fair,* a sophisticated intellectual magazine, ran a startling paper-doll series in the 1930s by Constantin Alajalov, a cartoonist and illustrator for, among others, Cornelia Otis Skinner. Alajalov lampooned J. P. Morgan, Albert Einstein, Ernest Hemingway, and Aimee Semple MacPherson as paper dolls. This series is the forerunner of the hundreds of editorial pages which used paper dolls to show the changing roles of women, the many activities of Henry Kissinger, and any other subject with many aspects.

Newspapers were printing a great many paper dolls, often in color, of the same flimsy stock used for the regular pages. Their natural subjects were characters from the comic strips in the same papers. Syndicated characters from Alley Oop appeared as paper dolls in 1937, Blondie came along in 1938, Dixie Dugan in 1939. A character called Flapper Fanny ran in 1936, while the

as Margaret Hays was out, and the modern angularity of Honti was in. Honti, a fashion illustrator for *Vogue* magazine, was a daring choice for a paper-doll assignment with the more mass-appeal *McCall's.* Ten Honti pages ran in 1925

and 1926, filled with the step-ins, uplift bras, and boudoir accessories of the period.

Interesting as his drawings were, they failed to attract and hold children's attention the way the more romantic fairy-tale figures or celeb-

The Ladies' HOME JOURNAL
22
June, 1923

The Poodle that Didn't Know English

Illustrations by Gertrude A. Kay

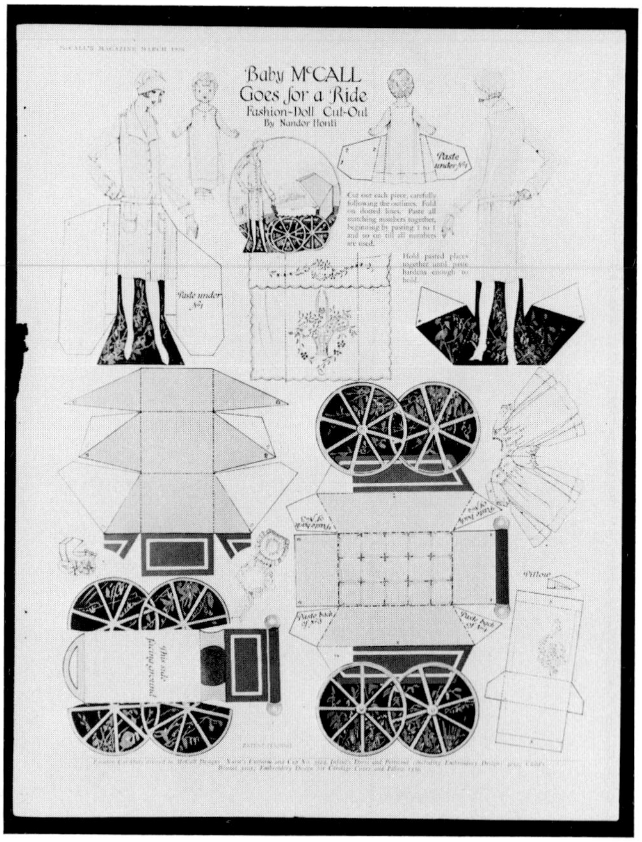

Baby McCALL
Goes for a Ride
Fashion-Doll Cut-Out
By Nandor Honti

THE BETTY BOBBS FAMILY
Pictorial Review for May, 1923
Betty's older sister Bonnie Bobbs
Drawings by Orpha Klinker

Peggy Pryde's Athletic Brother Phil

(*Top left, facing page*)
Gertrude A. Kay, a well-known illustrator of children's books, created these fanciful paper dolls for a story in the 1923 *Ladies' Home Journal*.

(*Top right, facing page*)
Nandor Honti's unusual Art Deco cutouts graced the pages of *McCall's*, 1926. Baby McCall and her carriage were elaborate two-sided figures.

(*Bottom left, facing page*)
Orpha Klinker's Betty Bobbs was the inspiration for Betty Boop. She is a curiously Art Deco period piece; *Pictorial Review*, 1925.

(*Bottom right, facing page*)
Pictorial Review also featured a series called Peggy Pryde. Her "athletic brother Phil" has the large waiflike eyes that anticipate a later vogue; 1926.

(*Above*)
No style in paper dolls proved as enduring as the sentimental, and *Pictorial Review* had a winner in Gertrude Kay's Polly Perkins series. Polly made a darling flower girl at her aunt's wedding, 1933.

(*Above right*)
Emma Musselman's soft watercolor drawings capture a romantic essence, as in this 1920 page from *Woman's Home Companion* introducing Margery May.

(*Bottom right*)
Musselman's lovely Tamaki, Margery May's friend, a Japanese paper doll with both Japanese and Western clothes; *Woman's Home Companion*, 1921.

Tillie the Toiler, a comic-strip
character, as a newspaper paper doll.
Her costume was supplied by a reader;
c. 1940.

vastly popular Flash Gordon characters ran in 1934 through King Features Syndicate. Jane Arden was a
1935 series, and included designs
sent in by readers. Tillie the Toiler,
Toots and Caspar, Popeye, and Little Orphan Annie are immortal
comic-strip characters for anyone
who grew up in the thirties. Along
with Winnie Winkle, Stella Clinker,
and Sophie Hoofer paper dolls, they
were avidly collected. A standard
format developed: they usually
came in a square panel as the last
box of a comic strip, often using the
home-drawn designs readers contributed for the joy of seeing their
designs and names in print.

A record of the times is clear in
these fragile little newspaper dolls.
The small, crudely printed figures
are often found with the original
two or three costumes, plus huge
handmade wardrobes designed by a
child. Only in the tight-money climate of the 1930s would any child

have worked so hard on such tiny,
flimsy drawings and saved them
with such care. As in the earlier
homemades, these dolls had clothes
made from wallpaper samples or
from color printing cut out of magazines. They were free playthings
when toys were hard to come by.

Walt Disney began making ani-
mated cartoon films during the Depression. The Disney characters
were regularly issued along with the
movies by the highly enterprising
Disney Enterprises. Disney produced Snow White, the Three Little
Pigs, Mickey Mouse, Ferdinand,
and Pinocchio in promotional paper
dolls that reminded children of their
beloved movies and encouraged
them to buy tickets.

Paper dolls continued to be in-
spired by childrens' books. Char-
lotte Henry produced a beautiful
Alice in Wonderland set in 1933.
Gulliver's Travels appeared in 1939,
Peter Rabbit in 1934, Raggedy Ann

and Andy in 1935, and Christopher
Robin by Queen Holden, in 1935.
The free library system was flour-
ishing, the literacy rate was high,
and even without the inexpensive
paperback book children managed
to get through a great deal of excellent reading. One Harvard graduate
is on record as stating that he had
read three-quarters of the great
books in a lifetime of reading before
he was thirteen. This was not unusual before the age of movies and
television. Children who knew the
stories were glad to have cutout versions of the characters for play, and
when they had acted out their heroes' original adventures went on to
invent new ones.

In addition to the ten-cent book,
commercial paper dolls came in
more expensive boxed sets, in the
nineteenth-century tradition. The
Samuel Gabriel Company, founded
in 1907 by the American representa-
tive of Raphael Tuck and Sons, produced many beautiful boxed sets,
varying in style from the "My Dolly" series to artist Betty Campbell's
up-to-date illustrations for "The
Costume Party" and a handsome
colonial Williamsburg family.
Compared to the booklets these sets
were expensive, and they did not
sell as well. But because they came
in their own containers more have
been saved in complete form, and
you may be able to acquire some at
fairs or in antique shops.

Taste was high even for inexpensive paper dolls in the thirties and
early forties. Rachel Taft Dixon, an
accomplished artist, drew magnificent sets of dolls from *Little Women*
and *The Five Little Peppers,* as well
as "Historic Costume" and "Peasant Costumes of Europe" paper
dolls. In a style typical of thirties'
children's books, Dixon drew detailed pictures of actual costumes or
used prints and paintings for reference. Forty years later, the Costume
Institute of New York's Metropolitan Museum of Art showed an im-

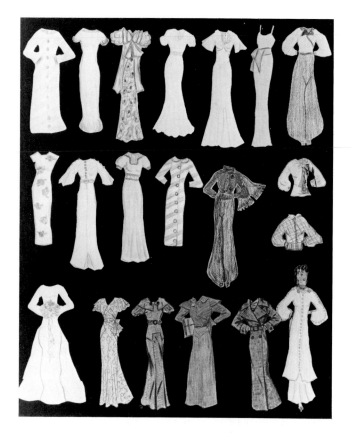

Dixie Dugan, another newspaper doll, and her enormous wardrobe. During the Depression children worked hard to cut out flimsy drawings like these; c. 1939. (The McNaught Syndicate).

Queen Holden's winning drawing of Christopher Robin, surrounded by his Pooh friends; Stephen Slesinger Inc., 1935. (*Reprinted with permission of Curtis Brown Ltd., London, on behalf of the Trustees of the Pooh Properties*).

portant group of peasant costumes, and almost every garment seemed familiar to anyone who had played with Dixon's set as a child. Paper dolls like these developed a feeling in children for costume and fashion, raising their taste level and encouraging them to learn more.

Some publishers of hard-cover children's books adopted paper dolls for stories from history or foreign travel. The Williamsburg Restora-

Rachel Taft Dixon drew memorable paper dolls based on characters from *Little Women* and *The Five Little Peppers;* 1941. (*Samuel Lowe Company, Inc.*).

Dixon also drew this magnificent set of "Historic Costume" paper dolls, whose accuracy was assured by her painstaking historical research; Whitman, 1934. (*Western Publishing Company, Inc.*).

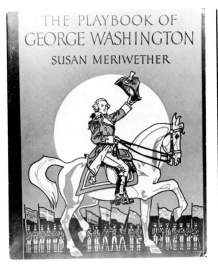

Paper dolls were used to teach history, as in this set devoted to the father of his country; 1928. (*Harper & Row, Publishers, Inc.*).

tion issued a pair of beautiful paper dolls in authentic costumes, with detailed information on the style and customs of the American colonial period. Many children, especially those in small towns without access to great museums, used paper dolls by good artists as well as book illustrations to help develop their taste for the fine arts.

Far more common, of course, were the paper dolls made to resemble pretty children. These were pouring out of commercial presses and being bought by millions of little girls. The same children enjoyed playing with paper houses and furniture. Always popular as a dollhouse substitute since paper toys began, sets of houses continued to record their times. There were also a great many cut-and-paste books filled with paper furniture. But a many little girls preferred to make elaborate scrapbooks of their own by cutting out magazine pictures and arranging them to please their

The Williamsburg Restoration Foundation issued this handsome pair of eighteenth-century fashion dolls in 1939. The dolls were accompanied by articles containing detailed period-fashion information. (*The Colonial Williamsburg Foundation.*).

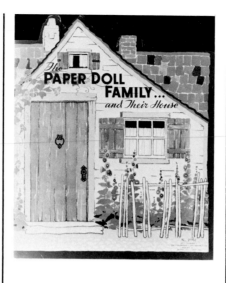

This typical paper doll has no special meaning, context, or historical connection. She's just the kind of pretty little girl that most children liked best; U.S., c. 1934.

Paper-doll houses proved popular, reflecting ideals of living conditions and fashions; 1934. (*Saalfield Publishing Company*).

Dolly, a paper-doll advertisement for Kellogg's Cereals, changed products with her dresses. The promotional message was on her back; c. 1935. (*Kellogg Company*).

own taste. If you should come across one of these homemade scrapbooks, you will find a treasure of nostalgia. Many were so detailed that children made cupboards with doors that opened to reveal paper products cut from advertisements, or filled closets with clothes cut from fashion magazines.

Paper dolls from the twenties and thirties are the easiest to find and buy, if you look carefully and are willing to be patient. They were issued in great number, considered precious enough to preserve, and were usually printed on good paper. Stay alert at fairs, flea markets, antique shops, and other outlets for

memorabilia, ephemera, and advertising giveaways. If you familiarize yourself with the drawing styles of the period and the characteristics of different artists by looking at magazines in your local library, you will readily recognize the same sorts of drawing in paper dolls. And if you are willing to buy cut pieces as you

Peggy Lux, a cartoon turned paper doll, knows the value of washing "her feathery rabbit's-hair undies" in Lux; c. 1935. (*Lever Brothers Company*).

The wedding was the most popular paper-doll event. Lucille Webster's set is a glorified version with 10 dolls and 120 pieces; 1935. (*Merrill Publishing Company*).

Hollywood was a potent influence on paper dolls. This set uses generalized portraits in place of "authorized" star pictures, but the clothes are the last word in style; 1939. (*Saalfield Publishing Company*).

An idealized "typical" American family—mother, father, six children, and maid—immortalized by Queen Holden; Whitman, c. 1931. (*Western Publishing Company, Inc.*).

discover them and assemble your own sets, you can have a fine collection for a very small cash outlay.

Dealers and mail-order sellers of paper dolls know all these sets by name, and can often identify every piece in them. They turn up on paper-doll lists again and again, although prices are rising rapidly. Dolly Dingles, which sold in 1975 for $3 each, now list at about $15 apiece. All the artifacts of the Depression years—glass, Fiesta ware, boudoir dolls, and the like—are rising quickly in price. But paper dolls, cheap to start with and worth nothing intrinsically, have remained affordable to almost everyone. The increases in Shirley Temple dolls of the same period are far more startling; a 1934 doll costing $2.98 sold for $600 in 1980.

Learn to riffle through piles of old magazines. Paper dolls in them may be intact and can be yours for the price of the magazine issue, rather than as a specialty item from a dealer. You may be lucky enough to find a cut set carefully stored away and kept flat in an old magazine.

If you hear of a warehouse sale, a fire or garage sale, or even an auction of old junk, go and watch for paper dolls. Many batches of unsold books have been bought for junk prices and picked up fresh as new by collectors. Sometimes a company that made advertising paper dolls will come across a batch of unmailed material and offer it for sale in the classified columns of newspapers. Dealers in elegant antique shops, if you have the courage to ask them, frequently have paper dolls in their storerooms or at home. If you collect paper dolls you must forget embarrassment and be ready to ask, poke about, insist, and get your hands dirty from old paper. You must also not mind being thought a bit peculiar. Meryle Evans, writing on ephemera for *Antiques World* in November, 1979, quotes a remark made to Bella C. Landauer, whose vast assemblings of trash formed the basis for the New-York Historical Society's collection: "I hear you are only collecting from scrap baskets." Paper-doll collectors all collect from scrap baskets.

The paper dolls of the 1940s continued to mirror their times. The movie influence endured and grew. The interest in families of paper dolls kept up, but the families changed with the times. In thirties books, families had fewer children and fewer aunts and cousins. The groups of servants disappeared, although the maid was a common fixture. It reminds us that in those days of high immigration and low domestic wages, middle-class families frequently had a maid. But even in the paper-doll world, she was a maid-of-all-work, with a dress for her day off, instead of the cooks, pages, nurses, and lady's maids of an earlier day.

World War II brought dramatic changes to everyday American life, and paper dolls faithfully reflected them.

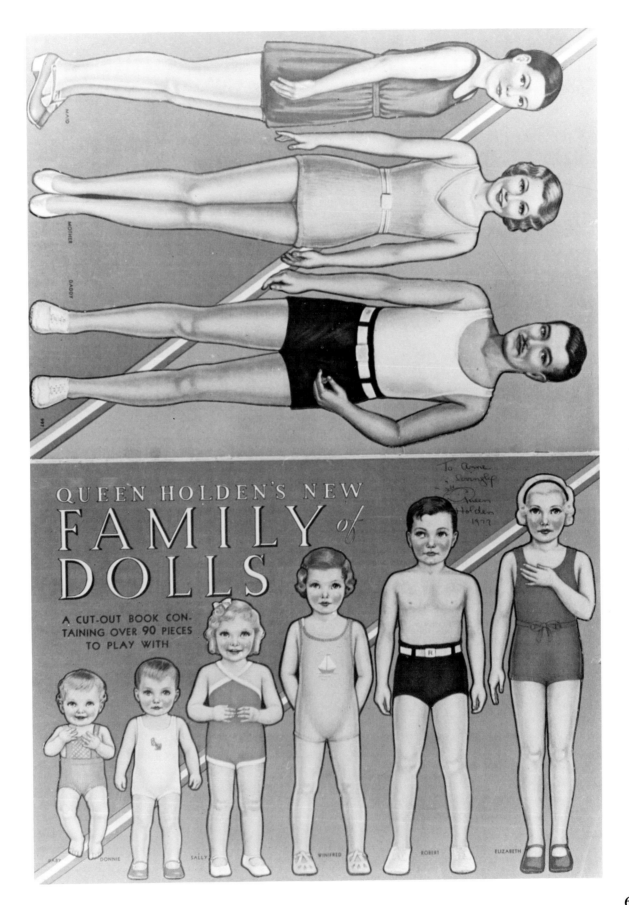

6

Paper Dolls Go to War

The 1940s were peak years for paper dolls. The way of life and the clichés that they pictured were the American way that young men were fighting for. Even the Hollywood stars most frequently portrayed in paper dolls became the pinup pictures of soldiers overseas.

Nearly every successful movie star became a paper doll in the forties. Deanna Durbin's paper wardrobe records the latest look for the ingenue: modest skirts, sweaters, and saddle shoes, feminine ruffles and frills for evening. It is hard for a teenager of the 1980s to imagine a wardrobe with so many dresses and so few comfortable pants. Jeans had not yet taken over the young fashion world; in the forties, pants were news when Marlene Dietrich wore them for evening. Most women never considered wearing pants except for camping or sports. Even for housework, the shirtwaist dress was the rule.

Movie-star paper dolls of the forties record the most beloved celebrities. Claudette Colbert, Judy Garland, Greer Garson, Ava Gardner, Gloria Jean, Betty Grable, Dorothy Lamour, Rita Hayworth, Hedy Lamarr, Jeanette MacDonald, Carmen Miranda, Mary Martin, Elizabeth Taylor, Lana Turner, Linda Darnell, Tyrone Power and Bob Hope, formed a sort of American royalty. Movie magazines filled with studio publicity told fans the smallest details of the lives of their favorites, advised women about copying stars' beauty secrets, and followed Hollywood romances, real and imaginary, in endless sequence. With paper dolls still selling for a dime, little girls could act out the lives of their favorite stars as they played at home.

Movie-star books continued to have captions, but they became less complex and more playful. "Puttin' on the Ritz" headlined an evening outfit, "Crankin' up rhythm" captioned a dance outfit, and, in the genuine slang of the day, "Two mug-bugs havin' some hoy toy toy."

Black-and-white studio pictures continued to fill the pages of paper-doll books, as well as thumbnail sketches of the stars wearing the clothing pictured. Pages were crammed with minute accessories like hair bows, snoods, bracelets, veils, handbags, roller skates, ice skates, and pillbox hats. Every jewel that Bette Davis wore as Queen Elizabeth was pictured for cutting out. Any girl who played with these dolls remembers the challenge of cutting out these little pieces without slipping, and of keeping them stored with the clothing. Today these same pieces keep collectors busy trading, identifying, mending. In fact, the accessories of forties books often makes collectors willing to pay twice as much for an uncut book as for the cut dolls. It takes tremendous patience and visual memory to get a set complete once it has been cut out.

Movie-star paper dolls showed everyday wardrobes in addition to the most famous of the star's costumes. All the books were excellent movie promotion, and all are excellent records of the Hollywood

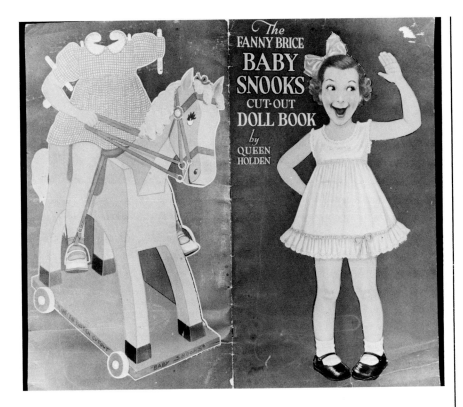

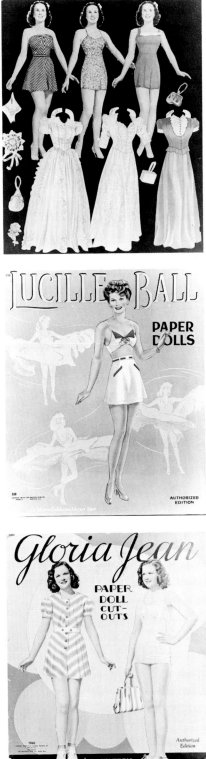

star system. In an era when few women owned a great number of clothes and fewer still owned glamorous ones, these books are little monuments to many women's dreams.

Specific movies provided material for paper dolls, as well. In 1940 *Gone with the Wind* thrilled audiences all over the country with its exciting stars and sweeping photography. The movie's place in film history can be judged from the fact that Merrill issued two authorized editions based on it.

The *Gone with the Wind* paper dolls are the aristocrats of movie paper dolls. In 1976 each sold for as much as $400, and the prices have risen since. If you know anyone who has saved one or preserved the cut dolls, you already have the basis of your paper-doll collection.

Not only famous movie stars, but also up-and-coming starlets, were used in paper-doll design.

Fanny Brice's irrepressible radio character Baby Snooks as a Queen Holden paper doll; Whitman, 1940. (*Western Publishing Company, Inc.*).

The ingenue, 1940s style: fresh-faced Deanna Durbin paper dolls; 1940. (*Merrill Publishing Company*).

Lucille Ball in her pre–"I Love Lucy" days was a glamorous M-G-M star who made a fine paper doll; 1945. (*Saalfield Publishing Company*).

"Movie Starlets," a 1946 set from the Whitman Publishing Company, shows Gail Russell, Diana Lynn, Olga San Juan, Marjorie Reynolds, and Joan Caulfield. The attrition rate of the starlet system is clear from the fact that only two of these women emerged in the fifties as paper dolls with booklets to themselves—Diana Lynn and Joan Caul-

Gloria Jean, also a 1940s movie star, in an "authorized edition" drawn by Bill and Corinne Bailey, 1941. (*Saalfield Publishing Company*).

BETTY
GRABLE

(*Above left*)
From the inside pages of several movie-star paper-doll sets, a plethora of accessories; U.S., c. 1943.

The most successful movie of its time, *Gone with the Wind* inspired two authorized versions from Merrill in 1940. One had two dolls of the stars, Vivien Leigh and Clark Gable, with one doll of teenager Ann Rutherford (Scarlett O'Hara's younger sister). The costumes are completely accurate, down to Scarlett's famous green velvet gown made from her mother's drapes. Demand was so great that the second set was issued, this one with eighteen characters (including two who had been cut from the film before its release). Different artists drew the adults and children, the latter the work of Miriam Kimball. (*Merrill Publishing Company*).

Pinup queen Betty Grable and her trunkful of Fifth Avenue clothes; Whitman, 1942.

Even Shirley Temple grew up and paper dolls kept an "authorized" record. Shirley's face is taken from a photograph; 1943. (*Saalfield Publishing Company*).

Another famous 1940s girl grew up to become Queen Elizabeth II. Her playhouse, apparently in the shadow of Windsor Castle, made a cutout story book; Dean & Son, London, c. 1953.

field. Like the star booklets, this set has studio photographs, decorative sketches of film reels, and accessories, along with the rich wardrobes of furs and glamorous gowns. As the styles of the 1940s are revived in the thrift-shop look of the 1980s, these paper dolls, with their shoulder pads, short skirts, and bias-cut gowns, begin to look quite new again.

But even the finest illustration techniques, like those done by Queen Holden for Judy Garland and Fanny Brice, seemed less interesting to audiences than photographs. Movie magazines, film itself, and the great photographic treasures in *Life* magazine were changing public taste. Advertisements, previously almost always illustrated, relied more and more on photographs, and new experts appeared with new

Paper dolls based on the dolls of princesses Elizabeth and Margaret Rose were dressed in clothes, including an ermine cape, by "famous fashion designers of France"; Whitman, 1940.

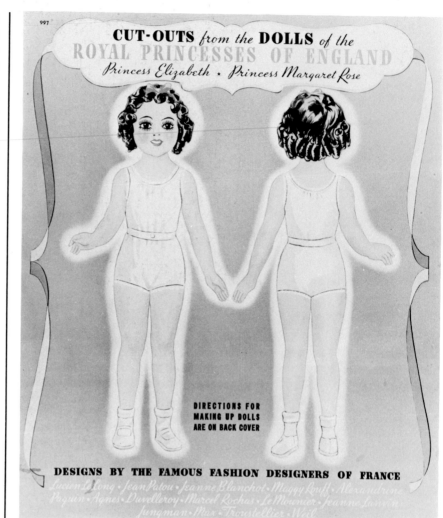

72

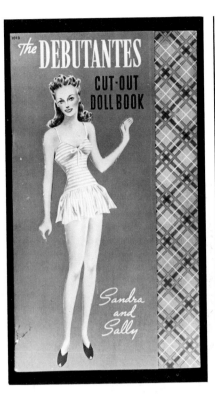

Between child and adult, the adolescent came into her own in the 1940s. Junior miss became a key fashion marketing concept, as well as a paper-doll subject; 1942. (*Saalfield Publishing Company*).

Paper dolls gave a glimpse of how the other half lived. This doll's angular, well-bred face identifies her as a debutante; Whitman, 1942.

photographic ideas each year. Magazine editorial pages filled up with photographs, and even lettering styles became simpler, lost their elaborate flourishes, and progressed to more readable phototype.

Fashion was taking giant steps in the forties, and sales techniques were growing more sophisticated every year. Mass clothing had been made either for adults or for children; the day a boy got out of short pants into long trousers marked his growing up, and girls looked either like children or women. But by the 1940s, psychology had identified the special qualities of the adolescent, and fashion discovered the junior miss as a selling concept. The term was made familiar to the public by Sally Benson's *New Yorker* stories, which eventually were turned into a hit play and movie. Just as in the eighteenth-century there were only infants and miniature grownups in the world of costume, the early twentieth-century recognized chil-

dren and grownups. But in the forties teenagers became a group with attitudes, problems, opportunities, music, and dance of its own. As the median age of the American population shifted downward, youth culture grew more important than ever. In the forties little girls waited impatiently to dress like their mothers. By the 1960s, mothers copied the clothes worn by their young daughters; the miniskirt, blue jeans, and T-shirts of the young became everybody's clothing.

When America entered World War II, all other concerns were secondary to winning the war. Paper, like many other commodities, was in short supply, and government regulation controlled its use. Paper-doll booklets of the war years had thin covers, no perforation, and used cheap paper. Magazine paper-doll pages disappeared. Editors were reluctant to spare precious space for children when there was so much to tell their prime readers. Of

all the magazine paper dolls, only Betsy McCall survived World War II. The children's magazines kept running paper dolls, but the ones in adult books disappeared. During the war, V-mail (in which letters were miniaturized photographically), the condensed book with small type, and the paperbound book with pages printed almost out to the margins were developed to meet the paper shortages. Paper-doll books suffered; the idea of wasting a precious substance by cutting it up for play seemed unpatriotic.

Still, paper dolls went to war with the materials left to them. The record of World War II paper dolls is one of the most interesting of all. Books based on military ideas were published by all the big paper-doll manufacturers, and were enormously popular. The uniforms pictured were entirely authentic, and often very detailed.

A large set by the Pachter Company in 1943 called "Ten Beautiful

This set of Robin Hood and Maid Marian paper dolls was printed on cheap paper and the figures were not perforated; 1956. (*Saalfield Publishing Company*).

"Smash the Axis" appealed to boys. It lampooned Hitler, Tojo, and Mussolini and included a surprise-attack fleet, tank, planes, and sailors; Electric Corporation of America, 1943.

Paper dolls join the war effort; "Victory Volunteers," 1942. (*Merrill Publishing Company*).

World War II brought back uniformed paper dolls. This pilot and stewardess stand in front of a fanciful rounded airplane; 1941. (*Merrill Publishing Company*), (*facing page*).

Girls in Uniform" held "90 large pieces, 25 complete uniforms front and back, in full realistic colors, also history of girls in service." The book listed nine services open to women in World War II; WACS, Marines, WAVES, SPARS, Army Nurse Corps, Red Cross, WOWS (Woman Ordinance Workers), Navy Nurses, and WASPS. There were military cutout toys for boys,

too, but by this time paper dolls were decidedly a girl's interest. "Smash the Axis" and other martial cutout books attempted to interest boys, but the great bulk of wartime paper dolls was aimed at American girls.

By 1943 there were many paper dolls in uniform from all the publishers, and girls too young to join up eagerly bought them. Hilda Kane and Wilma Miloche created five sets of children in uniform. Margaret Voight did a paper-doll set in which each of six children's names begins with one of the letters in the word UNITED. These books fairly shine with wartime patriotic enthusiasm.

Not since the Victorian era had paper dolls included so many uniforms. The earlier ones were all male; the new idea of women's services fascinated teen girls with their dazzling opportunities. The uniforms themselves were designed by the finest names in American fashion. Cutting out the pictures, American girls were still using paper dolls to learn about the best in contemporary clothes. The military wedding as a concept for a paper-doll set met with instant popularity, in an idea that combined a traditional fascination with the new wartime theme. Cutout battle sets meant for boys were popular, too.

It seems fitting that a famous paper-doll page served to announce the end of the war in Europe to sophisticated American adults. Constantin Alajalov, whose work had appeared in the caricature paper dolls of *Vanity Fair* in the thirties, drew the *New Yorker's* cover for June 16, 1945. It shows a uniformed soldier smiling happily at a paper-doll wardrobe of civilian clothing that would soon be available again. Nothing communicated the promise of peacetime choice faster, even for *New Yorker* readers.

All the wartime sets are seen on dealer's lists, and can be bought at

Glamorous gowns were traded in for official uniforms in this set of "Navy Girls and Marines"; 1943. (*Merrill Publishing Company*).

WACS and WAVES paper dolls provided patriotic inspiration to girls on the home front; Whitman, 1943. (*Western Publishing Company, Inc.*).

reasonable prices. As a body of work, they are not as attractive as earlier celebrity or costume dolls, so their prices are relatively low. Fewer of each set were issued because of the wartime paper shortage, but col-

Victory on all fronts: "Air, Land and Sea" paper dolls; 1943. (*Saalfield Publishing Company*).

One of the most unstereotyped paper-doll sets of the wartime years was "Girl Pilots of the Ferry Command"—no frilly dresses for these fighters; 1943. (*Merrill Publishing Company*).

lectors do not seem as attracted to these stylized forties dolls as they generally are to celebrities and glamor girls. As a record of popular culture they are often a good buy and a fascinating study. At least one of these wartime sets belongs in any collection based on chronological sequence.

The wartime sets signal the beginning of the end for paper dolls. Technology affected every aspect of American life once the war ended. The invention of plastic altered every household article and changed the world of toys from dollhouses to model soldiers. Television, sophisticated color in films, and the

Even "Our Wave Joan" was not too young to serve her country; Whitman, 1943. (*Western Publishing Company, Inc.*).

Girls could emulate the fighting men overseas with their own paper-doll versions of pinup girls; 1945. (*Saalfield Publishing Company*).

That perennial favorite, the wedding, also took on a patriotic color, as in this military-style affair; 1943. (*Merrill Publishing Company*).

Constantin Alájalov's cover for the *New Yorker*, June 16, 1945, celebrated V-E day with a paper-doll motif which vividly depicted the joys of returning to multifaceted civilian life. (*The New Yorker*).

"Stage Door Canteen" paper dolls included a set of code flags which spelled out PAPER DOLLS; 1943. (*Saalfield Publishing Company*).

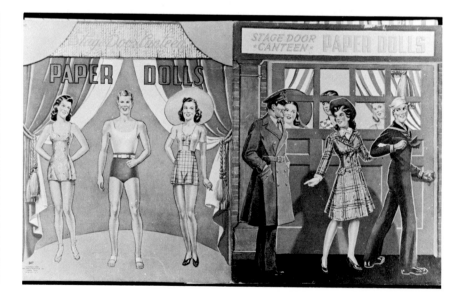

1555

Bride and Groom

6 Dolls and Clothes

Despite the fact that women had served in the armed forces and worked in factories, the postwar period showed a return to old sex roles. The only new aspect of this paper-doll bride is her Dior-inspired fashions; 1949. (*Merrill Publishing Company*).

increased superiority of all visual media contributed to the end of the paper doll as a precious plaything. Though they were sold in great number for another decade, paper dolls changed in the 1950s in more ways than ever before in their long history.

The wartime paper dolls signal the beginning of the end for paper dolls. Technology affected every aspect of American life once the war ended. The invention of plastic altered every household article and changed the world of toys from dollhouses to model soldiers. Television, sophisticated color in films, and the increased superiority of all visual media contributed to the end of the paper doll as a precious plaything. Though they were sold in great number for another decade, paper dolls changed in the 1950s in more ways than ever before in their long history.

The attitudes toward women were changing, too, though the full force of that change would not show for almost another decade. The war had put women in "men's" jobs, including factory assembly lines. Opportunities had opened that had been unthinkable before the fighting, and the effects of the changes reached down to little girls' play.

In 1949, Leonard Bernstein composed a symphony based on a poem by Auden, called *The Age of Anxiety*. By 1950, with traditional ideas changing fast, even paper dolls would show the effects of that anxiety, in a country no longer emotionally united by the single idea of winning a war.

7

Paper Dolls in the Age of Plastic

Once the wartime paper restrictions ended, paper-doll books came back in abundance. Their formats bacame fancier. Covers opened up in unusual ways, glossy cardboard appeared, "statuette dolls" of double-weight board came attached to the regular booklets. The number of celebrity sets printed in the ten years after the war was greater than those of any previous decade. The new dazzle was thought necessary by publishers partly because the ten-cent price for paper-doll books rose first to fifteen, then to twenty-five and even twenty-nine cents.

Glamor fashions and opulence returned once the war was over, and uniforms went into mothballs. Military paper dolls vanished. Nobody wanted to think about drab colors or plain fabrics; the wartime adage to "use it up, wear it out, make it do, do without," was forgotten. Movie and theater productions were expensively dressed and costumes were more lavish than ever. Paper dolls followed the trend.

The movie-star ideal had been changed dramatically by the war.

Servicemen coming home from fighting in Europe or the South Pacific seemed to want girl-next-door beauties, rather than the exotic prewar stars like Hedy Lamarr and Dorothy Lamour. The new ideal was typified by June Allyson, an all American girl; she and such wholesome stars as Julie Andrews, Pier Angeli, and Annette Funicello became the subjects of popular paper-doll sets.

A powerful new influence was growing quickly in the 1950s: television sets were being installed in more and more average homes, as the prices came down and the sizes of the screens went up. As always, paper dolls quickly reflected the new entertainment trend. TV stars turned up as paper dolls and were enormously popular from the start. Lucille Ball and Desi Arnaz as they appeared in "I Love Lucy," Gene Autry, Polly Bergen, Barbara Britton, and Giselle MacKenzie all starred in fancy paper-doll sets based on television shows. So did Mary Hartline ("TV's Golden Princess"), Jackie Gleason, and "The Honeymooners" cast, Ozzie

and Harriet, the Lennon Sisters, Dale Evans and Roy Rogers, Patti Page, Dinah Shore, and Walt Disney's Mouseketeers. The list gives a fairly comprehensive picture of which television shows were popular in the 1950s. It was quite a different kind of entertainment from any list put together in the thirties or even forties. The new star look began to force Hollywood to reexamine many of its traditional appeals, as producers searched for stars and subject matter to compete with the realism of television. And just as Tom Thumb and Jenny Lind recorded the trends of an earlier century in paper dolls, so the fifties sets documented their own time.

Paper dolls recorded events of the fifties. Princess Elizabeth of England became queen in 1953. To commemorate her coronation, which excited as much attention in the American press as it did overseas, Saalfield produced a handsome book combining coloring pages with paper dolls. Thousands of American girls listened to the broadcast of the ceremony in Westminster Abbey on short-wave radio

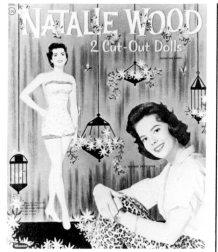

New movie stars emerged in the 1950s. June Allyson typified the girl next door, and her paper-doll figure was clothed in everyday outfits; Whitman, 1955.

Natalie Wood paper doll is surrounded by 1950s-style decor; Whitman, 1958.

Diana Lynn, a paper-doll veteran from her starlet days, got a set to herself; 1953. (*Saalfield Publishing Company*).

A regal beauty before she became a princess, Grace Kelly posed for this paper-doll set; Whitman, 1955. (*Grace de Monaco*).

and relived it with this set of paper playthings, directly in the tradition of the early Tuck figures of the English sovereigns.

Photography was used for more and more paper dolls in the fifties. *Life* magazine, having taught Americans to appreciate great photographs in an earlier decade, continued to support and promote new and startling photographic techniques. Children appreciated photographic portraits of their favorite stars as paper dolls.

Male stars were not neglected, and Rock Hudson personified the 1950s leading man; Whitman, 1957.

Television began producing celebrities in the 1950s; one of the first was the sleek Faye Emerson. Her facial expression was captured in the close-up version viewers recognized; 1952. (*Saalfield Publishing Company*).

A paper-doll bestseller showed everyone's favorite glamor girl, Marilyn Monroe, in black lace and swimsuit; 1954. (*Saalfield Publishing Company*).

Television and recording star Pat Boone made a homey paper doll; Whitman, 1959.

Even the torrid Jane Russell found her way to paper-doll treatment; 1959. (*Saalfield Publishing Company*).

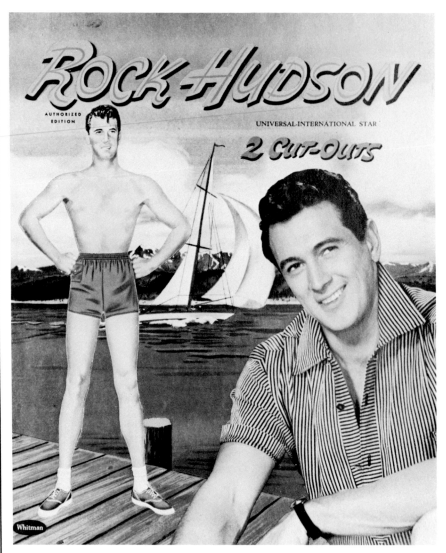

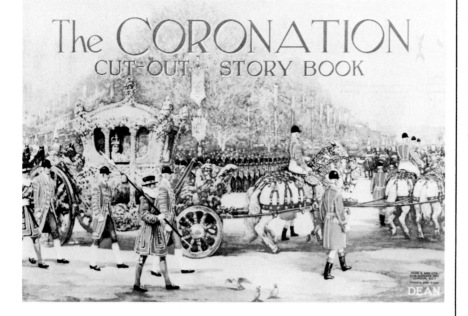

A cutout story book for a story-book event: the coronation of Queen Elizabeth II; Dean, 1953.

An American version of the coronation featured the queen, Prince Phillip, young Prince Charles, and baby Princess Anne, drawn from photographs and pictured in lifelike poses; 1953. (*Saalfield Publishing Company*).

One place where illustration remained popular was in the comic strip, which continued to provide a good share of paper-doll favorites. Bill Woggon's Katy Keene, at first a minor character in a 1946 strip, came into her own in 1949 and was published in comic books as an added feature through the 1950s and into the 1960s. Woggon also sold Katy Keene sets through the mail for ten cents. A good many of these bright paper dolls can be found in junk shops and at ephemera shows, with prices that rise steadily. In 1979 Marilese Flosser, a fashion coordinator at New York's Saks Fifth Avenue, reported on the influence of the original Katy clothes on designers. The clothes Katy wore look much like the nostalgic young fashions of the 1970s, and many young women adopted the Katy Keene look.

Although television seemed to have captured the child audience for magazine paper-doll pages (Betsy McCall is the one notable exception), the children's magazines kept printing them. *Children's Playmate* ran paper-doll pages, chiefly drawn by artist Fern Bisel Peat, through

In the Tuck tradition, Queen Elizabeth II is opulently presented in her coronation robe, coronation gown, and the robe of estate; *American Weekly,* 1953. Accuracy was necessary since millions of people around the world watched the ceremony on television.

Many magazine paper dolls ended with the rise of television, but not Betsy McCall, who managed to have a wonderful Thanksgiving; *McCall's,* 1951.

Elizabeth's Coronation Gown

BY SERGE FLIEGERS AND COMER CLARKE

PAINTED BY ANDRE DURENCEAU

In a room high over the dark circus of London sat a pretty young brunette—Queen Elizabeth II. And just like any other girl the world over, she faced a difficult problem: she had to make up her mind about a dress—the most important dress of her career.

Such a choice is not easy for a girl deciding on her first formal or the style of her wedding gown. But Elizabeth's problem was unique. She (Continued on page 26)

Elizabeth will be crowned with St. Edward's Crown.

Elizabeth's gown, shown at right, is made of shimmering ivory silk brocade and features gold, silver and diamante embroidery designs of British Isles emblems — roses for England, thistles for Scotland, leeks for Wales and shamrocks for Ireland.

Cap of Estate, worn early in ceremony.

Just before the new Queen receives St. Edward's Crown, she will put on gold and white robes of religious significance and cover them with this magnificent Dalmatic Coronation Robe of shining, pure gold cloth, decorated with roses and eagles.

Elizabeth will wear this Robe of Estate and the Cap of Estate when she enters Westminster Abbey to start coronation ceremony. The 20-yard train will be carried by eight attendants.

THE AMERICAN WEEKLY March 15, 1953 5

---

the 1950s. *Story Parade* featured paper dolls until it closed down in 1954. *Child Life* had a popular paper-doll series and so did *Wee Wisdom,* published for children by the Unity School of Christianity in Missouri. *Jack and Jill,* another favorite children's magazine, not only ran paper dolls but had stories and even poems about them, as well as articles on how to make and care for them. Starting in 1958, they ran a series on one hundred years of paper-doll history by Peggie Geiszel. The series reproduced simple versions of paper favorites from earlier times, including Taglioni and Dolly

Dingle. Still another children's magazine, *Children's Activities for Home and School* (later absorbed by *Highlights*), included paper dolls throughout the 1950s. Like the one featuring Eleanor Roosevelt, they were meant to inspire and educate children.

Curiously, all the subjects of children's-magazine paper dolls emphasize the themes common to early educational material in the same form. Costumes of foreign lands, famous people in history, and scenes of great moments in American life reappeared as teaching aids for the new generation.

Against the mainstream activities of its competition, *McCall's* inaugurated an enormously popular series, Betsy McCall, in 1951. It continued through 1974 on an almost monthly basis, and has been revived occasionally since. Betsy's activities document the interests of children in her time as precisely as the earlier Lettie Lanes and Betty Bonnets did. She was shown traveling to foreign countries, participating in American holidays, undertaking UNICEF collections, visiting sights such as New York's Metropolitan Museum of Art and Plaza Hotel, and busy fighting air pollution. Betsy McCall

Betsy McCall has
a wonderful Thanksgiving

HER MOTHER cooked the most enormous turkey you ever saw, and Betsy ate and ate and ate. "You'd better be careful," said her father. "You'll just blow up and bust if you eat another mouthful!" And her mother said, "You'd better save some room for dessert!" Betsy did, and she was very glad because dessert was McCALL's perfectly delicious ice-cream log. Then on Saturday Betsy went to a party at her cousin Barbara McCall's house. They had ice cream and cake and played games . . . Musical Chairs and Pin the Tail on the Donkey and hide-and-go-seek. And Betsy met a new boy named Jimmy Weeks. She likes him a lot.

This is Betsy's dress with the eyelet that she wore to the party

This is Betsy McCall and her little dog, Nosy

This is Jimmy Weeks, who has just come to live near Betsy McCall

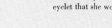
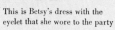

The paper hat that Betsy found in a cracker at the party

The dress that Betsy's grandmother gave her has lace and bows

This is the dress that Betsy wore for Thanksgiving dinner

166

has also helped to sell dress patterns and other related merchandise. Ginnie Hofmann is the artist responsible for Betsy McCall since 1958; the series was first drawn by Kay Morrissey between 1951 and 1955.

By this time, most paper dolls were frankly shown wearing underwear. A complete history of undergarments can be traced in paper dolls from their beginnings to the present. The figures must show a minimal shape in order to be a base

"Think pink" was a fashion phrase of the 1950s, and the new element in this otherwise traditional paper-doll wedding set; 1952. (*Merrill Company Publishers*).

A new frankness in portraying underwear is shown in two American Beauty paper dolls; (*Reuben H. Lilja Company*), c. 1950. It was anticipated by Queen Holden, in her drawings for these three lovelies; Whitman, 1942.

Designer Claire McCardell's paper-doll book was a showcase for her chic fashions. As the inside page reveals, her clothes were simple, unfussy, and elegant, and proved too advanced for those who favored a more sentimental approach to paper-doll wardrobes; Whitman, 1956.

for additional layers of paper clothing. Modesty prevailed for a hundred years; and even in the thirties, the bathing suit proved a perfect base for the celebrity figures whose dignity might have suffered if their photographs had been circulated in underwear. But after World War II pictures of women and men in their underwear seemed far less shocking. Marlon Brando in *A Streetcar Named Desire* had made a skivvy shirt seem the height of masculine splendor. Advertising for lingerie showed more details and more skin. The underwear that came out after the New Look had taken hold was synthetic; man-made easy-care fabrics were being bought by women everywhere to replace silks and cottons. Later paper dolls wore underwear still more minimal and would even be drawn in the nude, following the fashion of the times.

A paper-doll booklet that may represent the spirit of the 1950s better than any other is called "We're a Family." The American popular ideal in the prefeminist fifties was the family that lived happily in its own small house filled with labor-saving devices. Slogans like "the family that prays together, stays together" set the tone. *McCall's* coined the word *togetherness* as a promotional tool. The word came to symbolize precisely what families which had been separated by war wanted once the war had ended.

"We're a Family" gave a literal interpretation of the "togetherness" slogan of the 1950s. The paper-doll family was one piece, as were their outfits. Note the identical clothes worn by adults and children; Whitman, 1954; (*Western Publishing Company, Inc.*).

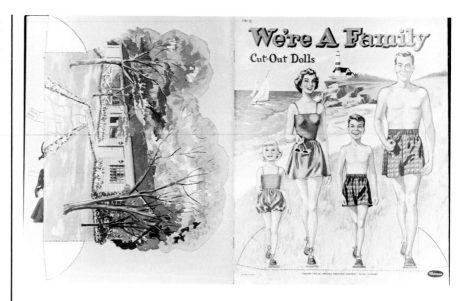

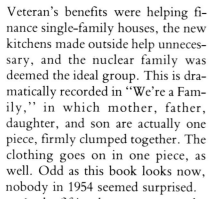

Veteran's benefits were helping finance single-family houses, the new kitchens made outside help unnecessary, and the nuclear family was deemed the ideal group. This is dramatically recorded in "We're a Family," in which mother, father, daughter, and son are actually one piece, firmly clumped together. The clothing goes on in one piece, as well. Odd as this book looks now, nobody in 1954 seemed surprised.

In the fifties there were new educational goals set for American children, and changes in conventional teaching. The country had time to concentrate on its children; schools began to be concerned with freedom from old disciplines, individual needs, and creativity. New reading methods and interesting ways to teach arithmetic were encouraged. Children no longer sat quietly at desks absorbing information. Dr. Spock and Dr. Gesell advised teaching children at varying speeds. Activities like cutting and coloring neatly no longer seemed best for children; free painting, fingerpainting, modeling with clay, gross motor play, and active sports were emphasized. Blocks grew bigger, dolls became unisex, old customs like teaching girls to sew and boys to work with wood began to disappear. The paper dolls little girls had loved for so long were not part of this new approach.

Even more important, plastic became available to the American child. Cheap, easily molded plastic proved ideal for dolls, soldiers, cowboys and Indians, doll furniture, and miniatures of all kinds. Once a little girl could own a real fashion doll, with a giant wardrobe of up-to-date clothing, paper dolls seemed far less interesting. And plastic dolls like Barbie could be dressed and played with the moment she was brought home. Paper dolls meant work. Since 1959, the Mattel Company estimates, more than 120 million figures of Barbie and her friends have been sold. We can pinpoint 1959 as the year when paper dolls as ordinary playthings began to die out.

The manufacturers did their best to meet the times and the competition. They invented the "punch out" doll, a simpler kind of paper figure that could be quickly pushed

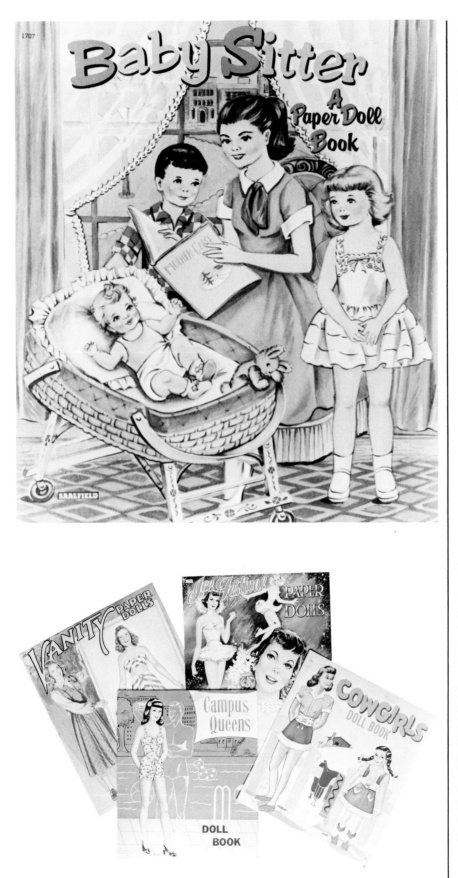

out of its page in one motion. Plastic was used for flat, two-dimensional dolls that could be dressed in clinging plastic clothes. But these cruder versions of paper play failed to change things. Paper dolls survived in a plastic world, but they were never again to be the same beloved playthings.

Plastic has replaced paper in a long list of ways familiar to ordinary people. Clothes that used to come from the dry cleaners wrapped in paper now comes in clear, strong plastic. Notebooks, food containers, carrying cases, and many more household objects that used to be made of paper are now familiar in plastic. Small wonder that paper dolls do not seem as interesting or natural for play among today's children.

By the 1960s, paper-doll publishers relied increasingly on television stars for the celebrity models. Paper-doll booklets dwindled, held far fewer outfits than ever before, and therefore had less play value. The 1930s books with twenty pages closely crowded with tiny accessories at a ten-cent cost vanished. In their place were large, simple paper-doll sets.

Television in the sixties produced paper dolls based on the cast of

Only exceptional (or exceptionally publicized) films inspired paper dolls by the 1960s. A case in point was *Cleopatra*, starring Elizabeth Taylor and Richard Burton. These dolls present a generalized image of Cleopatra and Mark Antony; Blaise Publishing Company, 1963.

Based on the television series "Julia," this set, featuring Diahann Carroll, was among the first to portray blacks in a glamorous manner and a welcome relief from the Aunt Dinah type; 1968. (*Saalfield Publishing Company*).

"The Beverly Hillbillies," Patty Duke, Richard Chamberlain (as Dr. Kildare), Sally Fields (as the Flying Nun), Carol Heiss, Shari Lewis, and Hayley Mills. Obviously their main attraction was the play tie-in with the shows, not intrinsic beauty, costume, or imaginative play value, as with the paper dolls of the past.

One of the sixties' most popular figures, Jacqueline Kennedy was the subject of a popular giant-sized paper doll. The clothes faithfully copy her wardrobe as First Lady, seen by millions in newspaper pictures and on television. The set was a special sort of paper doll with clothing that would cling, and it captured the chic of Jackie's inaugural gown, riding clothes, and pillbox hats. A matching set of Caroline Kennedy was also a popular plaything.

Although the Johnsons never were immortalized in paper-doll form, the Nixon women were available in paper. Interestingly enough, at the start of the 1980s dealers' lists show the Kennedy prices still going up, while the Nixon dolls were dropping.

Through the sixties and seventies, paper dolls were mostly relegated to the role of promotional material for Disney Productions, and for many television shows marketed for children. Girls who were young in the seventies often remember paper dolls as toys given them when

they were sick in bed. Children were interested in plastic dolls, hula hoops, skateboards, and plastic molding sets.

However, in the 1970s, a new phase of interest in paper dolls records still another popular trend, the new fascination for nostalgia. Inter-

The elegant Jacqueline Kennedy appeared as a paper doll when she was first lady, and her wardrobe was faithfully copied; Magic Wand, 1963.

The Nixon women also were made into paper dolls. Pat Nixon wears a modified miniskirt; 1969. (*Saalfield Publishing Company*).

A paper-doll based on Amy Carter promises "hours of fun"; Toy Factory, 1976.

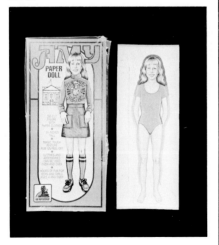

est in America's past was stirring up a number of trends in popular culture. Antique furniture, clothes, kitchen equipment, quilts, old objects of all kinds were suddenly sought after by the buying public. Prices for valuable antiques soared, and high prices were being paid for things formerly regarded as junk. Collectors seemed to appear in every possible category—barbed wire, glass insulators, matchbooks—and even paper dolls of the past. Auctions became bigger business than ever. Flea markets, fairs, ephemera shows, paper memorabilia shows, and toy fairs multiplied all over the

United States. Encyclopedias and books on objects of the past began selling in large numbers, with price guides revised each year to record new amounts being paid for old things. Courses were offered in adult-education centers on almost every aspect of finding, buying, and selling antiques and collectibles; magazines for women were filled with news of the antiques boom, and rapid inflation began to make collectibles seem like good investments.

Along with other trivia from the past, paper dolls moved into a new phase.

8

Antiques, Replicas, and Collectibles

By the 1970s paper dolls had come full circle: from their beginning as adult toys, through years as playthings for children, back to an adult interest. Variety, toy, and stationery stores still sold paper-doll booklets, at seventy-nine cents and up, but the paper dolls were different from those of twenty years earlier. The trends begun in the fifties and sixties resulted in new press-out books, which eliminated cutting out and made the dolls quick to get at, and in the increased use of photographic reproduction. In the seventies entire paper-doll booklets, not just the main figures, became photographs.

The Effanbee Doll Company sponsored sets using photographs of some of their popular dolls and clothes. *Storybook, Currier and Ives,* and *Gigi* paper-doll books are colorful modern playthings, particularly for children who love the plastic dolls. These paper dolls are advertised as suitable for use in doll-house rooms as "period doll-house occupants." The miniature buffs of the 1970s have made doll-

house decoration America's favorite hobby after stamp collecting, and such paper dolls naturally tie in.

Though not the big business it used to be, paper-doll publishing is alive and well, while definitely recording the shift from a childhood to an adult interest. Dover Publications has issued many paper-doll books and has plans for more. True to the nostalgia trend, the books are either reproductions of earlier material, like Barbara Jendrick's *Advertising Paper Dolls,* or new designs based on nostalgic themes, like Tom Tierney's *Pavlova and Nijinsky Paper Dolls.* The Dover list is long, and includes *Antique French Jumping Jacks,* based on the first *pantins; Erté Fashion Paper Dolls of the Twenties, Glamorous Movie Stars of the Thirties, Victorian Fashion Paper Dolls From "Harper's Bazaar" 1867–1898, Dolly Dingle Paper Dolls,* and many others.

Another publisher of beautiful new paper dolls is Bellerophon Books. Their *Great Women Paper Dolls,* featuring black-and-white

cutouts of Cleopatra, Eleanor of Aquitaine, Lady Murasaki, Florence Nightingale, Susan B. Anthony, and many more, is fascinating. Bellerophon also published *Infamous Women Paper Dolls,* which features Mata Hari and Lucrezia Borgia paper dolls, and sells handsome paper-doll versions of *Henry VIII and His Wives, Queen Elizabeth I, Sleeping Beauty Ballet Paper Dolls,* and others.

In addition, many artists are drawing beautiful modern paper dolls or designs based on earlier figures. Pat Stall, Pat Frey, Lou Valentino, Marianne Anderson, Carol-Lynn Waugh, Sandy Williams, Marilyn Henry, Winnie McKelvey, Loraine Burdick, Susan Sirkis, Lenore Kobayashi, Bruce Patrick Jones, Peggy Jo Rosamund, Paula Wolak, Emma Terry, and Fran Van Vynckt are some of the creators of modern paper-doll originals. Many of them began their art careers because of paper-doll collecting, and their example is fascinating. If you are an artist or a would-be artist, trying your hand

A selection of Dover paperback paper-doll books ranges from the nineteenth-century delights of *Godey's Lady's Book* and the *Victorian Parlour* to Erté 1920s fashion paper dolls, Rudolph Valentino dolls, and Marilyn Monroe dolls. The interest in paper dolls of the near and distant past is steadily growing. (*Dover Publications, Inc.*).

Bellerophon books has issued paper-doll books which feature Queen Elizabeth I, Henry VIII, American Revolutionary soldiers, and women famous and infamous. (*Dover Publications, Inc.*).

Something new in paper dolls: "Jewish" and "black" models intended as educational toys. The dolls come with stories of how minorities lived in the 1930s and 1940s. These realistically drawn figures would have been unthinkable in earlier times; 1977. (*Rinna Evelyn Wolfe: Lah-ti-da Creations*).

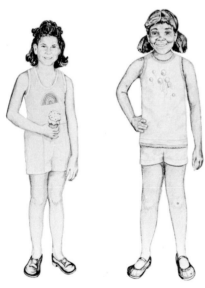

96

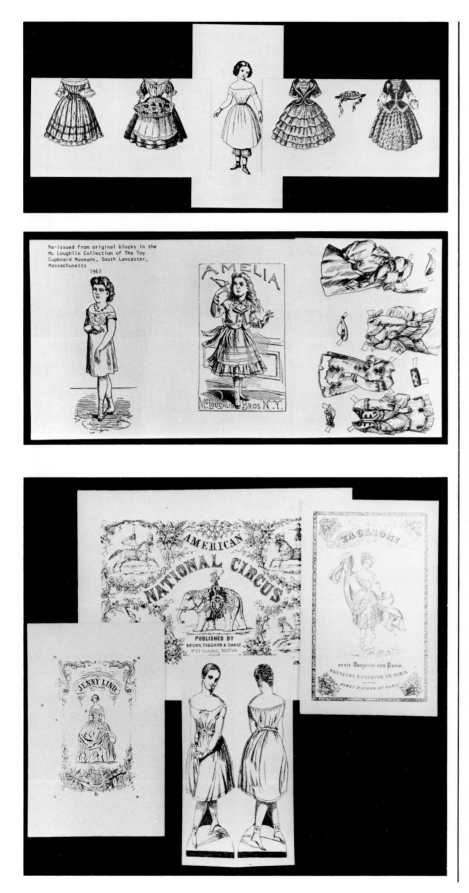

Herbert Hosmer's Toy Cupboard Museum in South Lancaster, Massachusetts, is a source of wonderful reproductions of antique paper dolls, including Carry, with "the latest Paris Fashion," 1857; Amelia, a McLoughlin doll; and such historic dolls as Jenny Lind (1845), Taglioni, and the American National Circus; 1952–1967. (*The John Greene Chandler Memorial Collection*).

at original paper dolls (or filling in missing parts of your collection) can be irresistible.

Western Publishing Company, of which the Whitman Company is now the children's book division, publishes paper dolls based on Barbie and Skipper, another popular doll. It also issues paper dolls based on cute characters called the Ginghams, Calico Cathy, Mattel's Itsy Bitsy Beans, as well as an attractive book called *Paper Dolls of Early America*. In 1970 the same publisher issued "Beth Ann" by Kathy Lawrence, Queen Holden's daughter. Similarities in the newer illustrations of endearing baby clothes and elaborate accessories make this book a collector's prize.

Jean Woodcock, a paper-doll expert from Tulsa, Oklahoma, bought the Merrill Company in 1980, and has plans for new issues of old favorites. The original art work for many famous paper dolls from Merrill and the other large companies is probably the most valuable class of collectible in the paper-doll world. Kent State University in Ohio owns the archives of the Saalfield Publishing Company and generously makes them available for collectors and nostalgia buffs to examine.

As early as the 1950s, a few collectors recognized the wisdom of reproducing valuable pieces. Replicas made about a hundred and fifty years after the originals are labeled "antique." The definition of an antique in terms of time has been condensing, as the world seems to change faster. Many Americans think of Tiffany lamps, Depression glass, Chippendale chairs, and Barbie dolls all as antiques.

By 1958, children's magazines had begun reprinting famous early paper dolls in black-and-white line drawings. Even earlier, in 1956, Herbert Hosmer, whose Toy Cupboard Museum in South Lancaster, Massachusetts shows the originals, issued black-and-white reproductions of the 1845 Jenny Lind paper dolls, complete with folders, a pamphlet detailing the history of the singer and the doll, plus instructions for accurately hand coloring the drawings. In 1957, Hosmer issued a similar copy of the Taglioni doll. He has also reproduced the American National Circus, a charming paper toy from the nineteenth century, as well as some early woodblock paper dolls. All these copies are themselves treasures for collectors.

A few American museums have also reproduced some of their paper treasures. The costs of color printing have risen so drastically in the century between original and reprint that most copies are black and white. But the Spring 1976 *Bulletin of the Metropolitan Museum of Art,* an issue given to paper ephemera, featured an Enameline advertising paper doll of the early 1900s on its cover, showed more of the series on inside pages, and contained a centerfold page with a color copy of a chromolithographed paper doll. The pages were sold separately as a sheet in the museum's shop. Blaise Castle House Museum of Social History in Bristol, England, has issued a sheet showing a famous 1840 paper doll, Psyche, with dress and bonnet. In Copenhagen, the National Museum sells a great many beautiful color sheets, most of them exact replicas of originals in the museum's possession. Collectors are lucky to find these attractive reproductions, infrequently printed and

available in limited quantities.

Dover has issued *Old Fashioned Cut-Out Paper Dolls,* replicas of 1900s originals in several sizes, as well as other antique dolls. The Scolar Press in London has replicated *Little Fanny* and *Little Henry* in charming editions. While these replicas are only a sample of what is available or will soon be available, they do show why collecting paper dolls is a foolproof hobby for beginners.

The untrained eye can easily tell an original paper doll from its rep-

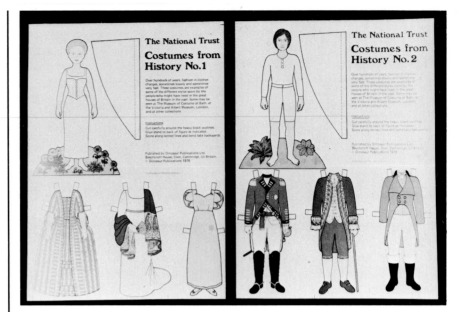

Britain's National Trust offers paper dolls with historically accurate costumes based on museum collections; 1976. (*Dinosaur Publications*).

lica. In copies, colors are muddier, borders are more blurred, the paper has a totally different feel. In addition, most replicas are carefully marked as copies, and many are even deliberately redone in different sizes from their original models. As costs of printing have mounted, printers estimate that it would cost approximately fifty times the origi-

98

No. 9742.

99

Figurer til Paaklædning.   Danske Billeder Nr 23.   Alfred Jacobsens Forlag Kjøbenhavn

No. 10182.

The Danes have shown a great interest in preserving and distributing historical paper dolls. The National Museum in Copenhagen reproduced these beautifully colored sheets of paper dolls (*also see preceding page*) from its collection. Reasonable prices; 1971, 1977.

nal outlay to reproduce an early paper doll exactly. This means that no one will be able to sell you a replica for the price of an original. Few other fields offer so much safety for new collectors. Experts are often fooled by furniture, china, even painting forgeries. But paper-doll experts are more easily made, and much safer.

Though comparatively few museums have reproduced paper dolls in their collections for sale, as the Copenhagen National Museum has

Dover Books has issued several books devoted to paper dolls of the late nineteenth and early twentieth centuries, and Scolar Press has reproduced the 1810 editions of *Little Fanny* and *Little Henry*. (*Dover Publications, Inc.*).

Merrimack Publishing Company has made available "exact replicas of museum collections" of late nineteenth-century paper dolls, complete with elaborate costumes and accessories. It has also published an antique replica of a cutout teddy bear. (*Merrimack Publishing Corporation.*).

ANTIQUE PAPER CUTOUT
DOLL & CLOTHES

EXACT REPLICA OF MUSEUM COLLECTION
of the LATE 1800'S

ANTIQUE REPLICA
CUT-OUT TEDDY BEAR
with Five Costume Changes, Two Hats

- Hours of imaginative fun-play. Costumes include: Dress Suit, Robe, Overcoat, Yachtsman, Baseball.
- Place costume on bear and fold tabs back. Slit on hat fits onto head.

© Merrimack Publ. Corp. N.Y. 10003 No. 9116 Printed in Hong Kong

done so lavishly, many have issued new paper dolls to display costumes in a form children will enjoy. The Cincinnati Art Museum sells a book of costume drawings in paper-doll form, and the Royal Ontario Museum has paper dolls on card stock created from pieces in its costume collection. In Great Britain, many National Trust shops sell cutout sheets of historical costume paper dolls, men and women in drawings from actual costumes or old paintings, men in armor, houses, cathedrals, and churches to cut and put together. The Victoria and Albert Museum in London sells three handsome folders of costume paper dolls. And in 1980, Carol Law's collage based on 1930s paper dolls was exhibited at New York's Cooper-Hewitt Museum.

The Wolfe Publishing Company in Great Britain issues beautiful books, written and illustrated by Richard Hook, of carefully researched costume paper dolls. The series has Elizabethan, Regency, Victorian, and Napoleonic costumes, as well as men in armor and in naval uniforms. These books are growing harder to find as paper-doll collectors snap them up to use in costume research.

Many of these replicas and modern costume paper dolls are being bought by adults rather than children. People who loved paper-doll play in their own childhoods pick

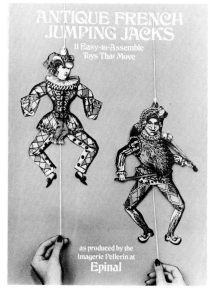

Dover has also issued replicas of antique French jumping jacks, which are, in fact, the *pantins* produced by the Pellerin family of Epinal; 1979. (*Dover Publications, Inc.*).

The use of paper dolls in advertisements continues to the present day. Bloomingdale's, one of New York's most fashionable retail stores, ran this paper-doll-style ad in *The New York Times* in 1979.

Maidenform Company capitalized on the connection between underwear and paper dolls in this advertisement. "I dreamed I was cut out for fun," the copy reads; 1958.

up such inexpensive reproductions as they find them. If you are one, the basis for a collection is already yours. But if, as often happens, you have given your treasures to a modern child, you will probably find that her interest is far less intense than yours.

For adults, too, are today's advertisements that feature paper dolls. In 1979, Bloomingdale's ran full-page advertisements in *The New York Times* using paper dolls as their theme. Eiderlon and Maidenform have used paper dolls to boost their sales, perhaps without realizing the long history of paper dolls as underwear advertisements.

Since the concept of the paper doll is so clear in adult minds, editorial art directors sometimes use it to convey the idea of a single person with varied roles. In 1974 *Time* magazine showed Henry Kissinger as a paper-doll figure in a page remi-

niscent of the Alajalov caricatures of the 1930s. Many editorial pages have hit on the idea of the paper doll as a way of showing the various and changing roles of women in society.

Avon Publishing Company helped publicize Gilda Radner in a sophisticated paper-doll set. Still more advanced is a set of homosexual male and female paper dolls called *Attitudes* by Tom Tierney, sold in bookstores throughout the United States. The popular Miss Piggy is a Muppets paper doll, complete with satin tap pants and a roller-disco outfit.

These are more or less adult paper dolls and ideas; unless the world dramatically changes course, plastic, television, and the new "creativity" in education all spell the end of paper toys. While they lasted, these bits and pieces faithfully reflected their worlds in happy sentiment and minute detail. Today's children pre-

fer electronic games, hundred-piece plastic doll houses, space-age weapons, and adult-look dolls with giant wardrobes.

Collectors see the change as a continuing record of the times, and work harder than ever to preserve old paper as samples of life in simpler eras. A small group of "paper dollers," as they call themselves, exists and grows, publishing newsletters, issuing ever handsomer quarterly magazines, industriously copying by machine unidentified paper dolls, writing one another voluminous letters, holding conventions, parties, and informal get-togethers, traveling, trading, buying, selling, and learning more all the time. The amount of time these collectors spend on paper dolls seems staggering, but it has produced bibliographies, long address lists of collectors throughout the world, painstakingly researched articles on the

103

smallest details of antique dolls, and more.

There are many ways to be interested in paper dolls. More people are discovering existing ones, and inventing new interests based on them, than ever before.

Time magazine reprinted Wright's 1974 cartoon from the Miami *News* showing Henry Kissinger's many roles in paper-doll style; the message was clear.

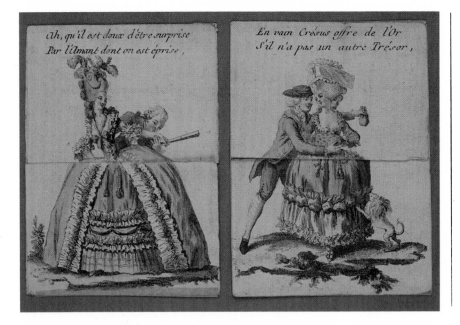

Ah, qu'il est doux d'être surprise
Par l'Amant dont on est éprise.

En vain Crésus offre de l'Or
S'il n'a pas un autre Trésor.

Two trick cards, c. 1785, popular as adult toys at the French court. The watercolor pictures change as the parchment cards open. At left, a fashionable lady is transformed into a shepherdess, in a masquerade like those Marie Antoinette and her ladies enjoyed; at right, a gentleman's love offering of gold turns into flowers.

Air, Des folies d'Espagne.
En vain on aime à voir dans une Glace,
Sa taille fine et ses traits merveilleux,
Si quelque Amant n'admire notre Grace,
Et ne nous vient offrir de tendres vœux.

Air, Des rigueurs de la St Agathe.
Je suis toujours tendre et sincère,
Vrai modèle de tout amant ;
Si j'ai le bonheur de vous plaire
Ah que mon sort sera charmant.

Air, Des folies d'Espagne.
En vain on aime à voir dans une Glace,
Sa taille fine et ses traits merveilleux,
Si quelque Amant n'admire notre Grace,
Et ne nous vient offrir de tendres vœux.

Air, Des rigueurs de la St Agathe.
Je suis toujours tendre et sincère,
Vrai modèle de tout amant ;
Si j'ai le bonheur de vous plaire
Ah que mon sort sera charmant.

Air, Il n'est qu'un pas du mal au bien,
Amans, n'aiez aucune transe,
En soupirant à qui mieux mieux,
Et soiez plus audacieux,
Que je ne parois quand je danse ;
En un instant il faut gagner,
L'Ame sur qui l'on veut régner.

Air, Dans un berger Colinette,
Aussi belle que la rose,
Faite pour charmer nos yeux ;
L'Une et l'autre à peine éclose,
Vos appas sont radieux.
Vous êtes sur toute chose,
Le vrai Chef-d'Oeuvre des Cieux.

An uncut, eighteenth-century pantin (*right*) represents the popular toys of aristocrats at the French court. Designed to be cut out and strung together, this paper courtier would dance when jounced up and down. Pantins were named for the Paris suburb where many were made, but were popular in other countries. They were called jumping jacks in England, hampelmenn in Germany, and fanucci in Italy. The forerunner of all activated paper dolls, this early example in watercolor is rare and beautiful. The general subject matter for pantins included milkmaids, shepherds, and the commedia figures, all undoubtedly safer than portraits in the changing political climate at the court of Versailles.

Early paper dolls were used as dressmaker's samples. This handmade doll (*below*), probably a likeness of a prospective customer, is called Miss Lascelles, Made in France c. 1798, she was later brought to England; she is six inches high, watercolor on paper. Her costumes are straight and simple, a reaction to the elaborate fashions of prerevolutionary France. Other hats must have existed but only the plumed turban survives.

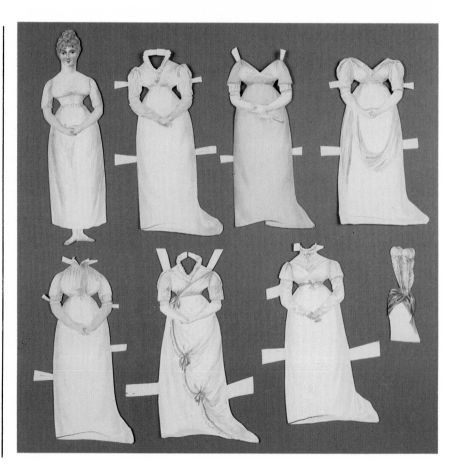

Two early paper dolls (*left and center*), dated 1791, London; the date and the engraver's name are worked into the design of each costume. The movable heads are on slender paper stands which the costumes cover. Four costumes survive for the woman, four for the man; they are minutely detailed outfits of a well-to-do couple. The figures were precut, scissors being too scarce and expensive to be used for toys.

The History of Little Fanny Exemplified in a Series of Figures (*bottom left*) was an instant success when published by S. and J. Fuller, London, in 1810. The moralizing tale of the naughty runaway who learns her lesson appealed to parents, but the charming cutouts attracted children.

Fuller was quick to follow his success with *The History and Adventures of Little Henry* (*bottom right*), 1810. The fanciful costumes detail Henry's progress from beggar to "future Nelson."

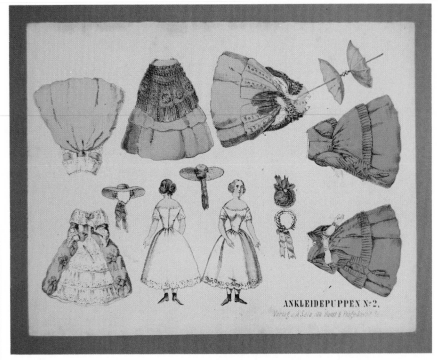

The Fuller books sold in England for six shillings, a considerable amount for a toy in 1810. European books had similar price tags. Since ordinary people could not afford them, many mothers copied out the verses from borrowed originals and painted their own figures. Handwritten and watercolored versions turn up occasionally, some with extra text, many even more charming that the printed originals like this 1811 copy of *Little Fanny* (*above*).

Germany produced sheets of paper dolls called *Ankleidepuppen* ("dress-up dolls") from about 1845, the approximate date of these examples. Devoid of moral instruction, they offered beautiful playthings for a girl who could cut out the ribbons, nets, and other tiny details.

Fanny Gray, an American version of *Little Fanny,* was published in Boston by Crosby, Nichols and Company in 1854. The doll was larger and her costumes more colorful than her English cousin's, and the book was a great success.

Clara (*left*) was among the first paper dolls sold in an envelope, a less expensive alternative to box sets that proved very popular. Clark, Austin, Smith, New York, c. 1858.

The Peter Thomson Company of Cincinnati devised a new form for paper dolls: a small screenlike folder which was economical to print flat. Mary Bell (*below*) dates from about 1855.

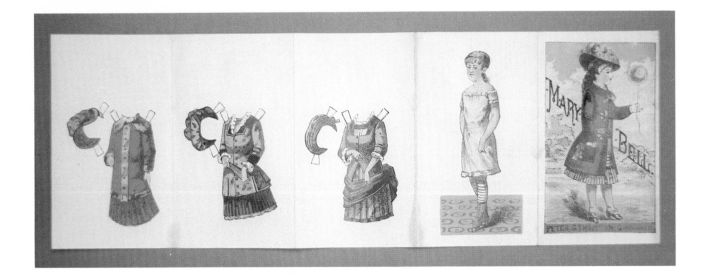

The first paper dolls known to have been inspired by a popular novel were characters from *Uncle Tom's Cabin*. Topsey, shown here in front and rear views, was also the first black paper doll. McLoughlin Brothers, New York, c. 1863.

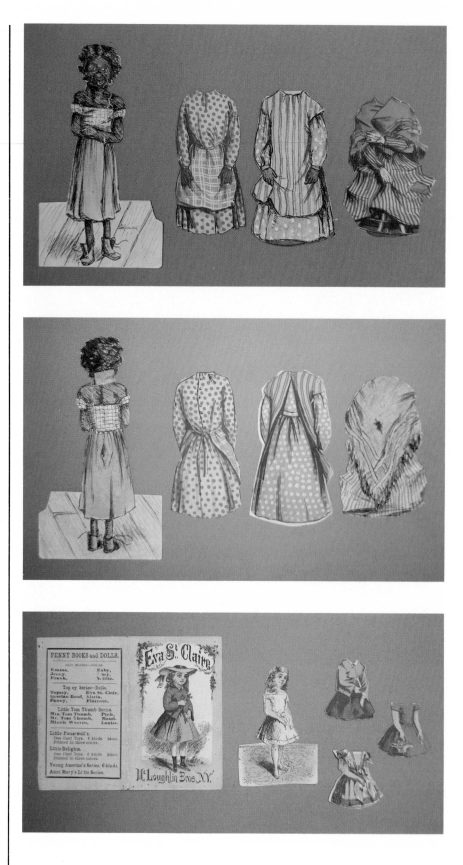

Little Eva St. Claire, from the same series as Topsey, shown with the cover of the booklet that contained her; McLoughlin, c. 1863.

Celebrity paper dolls were an early and lasting tradition. One of the first was this "little lady," Mrs. Tom Thumb, of the midget family made famous by P. T. Barnum. Her costumes are beautifully detailed and colored. McLoughlin, c. 1864.

McLoughlin produced the first mass-marketed paper dolls in America. Rosa Rustic and Kitty Black were both printed about 1870.

DIAGRAMS FOR DRESSING CHILDREN.—FOR LITTLE GIRLS WHO READ GODEY.

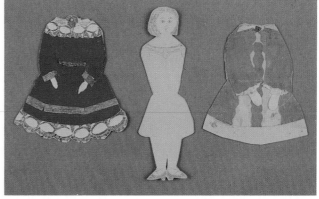

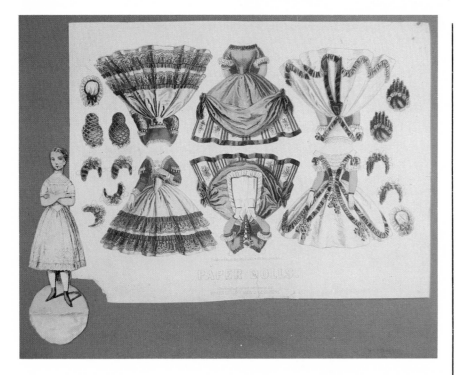

PAPER DOLLS.

A page of paper dolls from *Godey's Lady's Book* (*top left*), one of the most popular American women's magazines of the nineteenth century. The dolls date from 1859, the year Godey added them for the benefit of his readers' children.

A small homemade paper doll, (*top right*), U.S., c. 1865. Many girls made their own paper dolls and outfitted them with handmade dresses cut from scraps of fabric.

Some paper dolls from magazines were quite elaborate, as is this chromolithographed beauty from the pages of *Frank Leslie's Lady's Magazine* (*left*), c. 1866. Eliza Leslie was the fashion arbiter of her day. Costumes for the doll appeared in subsequent issues, thus boosting circulation.

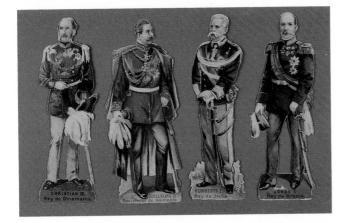

Pages from a scrapbook dated 1890, a Christmas gift from a Parisian mother to her child (*top left*). The paper figures, from the extraordinary workshop of Raphael Tuck & Sons, London, depict characters from Shakespeare's *Romeo and Juliet* and *Much Ado About Nothing*.

Winsome Winnie (*above*), a typical Tuck child, c. 1902. Tuck paper dolls frequently came in three sizes to attract a maximum number of buyers.

(see preceding page)
The most lavish Tuck productions were masterpieces of embossed, brilliantly colored paper figures; among the finest is this rare set of the rulers of the world at the time of Queen Victoria's Jubilee of 1887. The dolls, labeled in Spanish (suggesting a European-wide market), depict Christian IX of Denmark, Wilhelm II of Germany, Humberto I of Italy, George I of Greece, Oscar II of Sweden and Norway, Moutsuhito of Japan, Dom Luiz of Portugal, Kuanghsu of China, Dom Pedro II of Brazil, President Sadi Carnot of France, President Benjamin Harrison of the United States, President Hammer of Switzerland, Alexander III of Russia, Franz Joseph II of Austria-Hungary, the Prince of Wales (later Edward VII of Great Britain), Abdul-Hamid I of Turkey, Pope Leo XII, Leopold II of Belgium, Alfonso XIII of Spain, and Victoria of Great Britain.

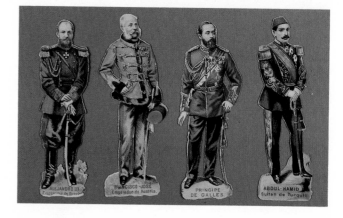

Another magnificent Tuck set, c. 1889, portrays the sovereigns of Great Britain in exquisite detail: John holds the Magna Carta, Richard the Lion-Hearted seems ready to join the Crusades, Richard III is suitably menacing, Elizabeth I is glorious, the stern Cromwell glowers, and Victoria brings the procession to an imposing conclusion. *(see next pages)*

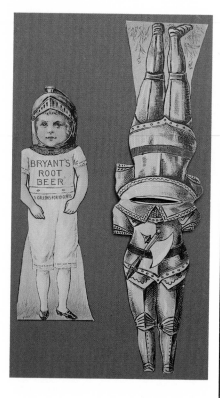

Manufacturers discovered that paper dolls could make attractive and effective advertisements. This little knight (*above*) is advertising Bryant's Root Beer, "five gallons for ten cents"; c. 1890.

McLaughlin XXXX Coffee issued this lovely back-and-front paper doll (*top right*) c. 1893; it is easy to imagine a little girl impatiently waiting for her parents to use up the coffee so she could add a new figure to her collection from the next bag.

A basketful of kittens in her arms, this paper girl (*right*) is an advertisement for the New England Mince Meat Company, c.1890. The copy on her back offers "the full set, 16 dolls all different," in exchange for ten fronts from the product's package.

Enameline Stove Polish issued dolls representing American colleges, a further inducement to collect the whole set (and buy more polish). This fellow is from Cornell, whose cheer is printed on his back; c. 1890.

A particularly handsome paper-doll set (*facing page*) was available in exchange for coupons from Durham Tobacco; c. 1895.

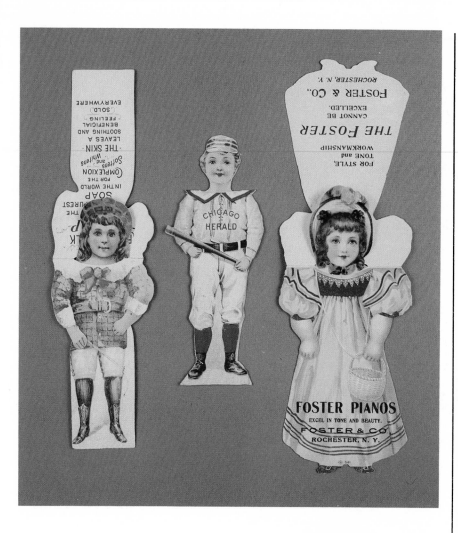

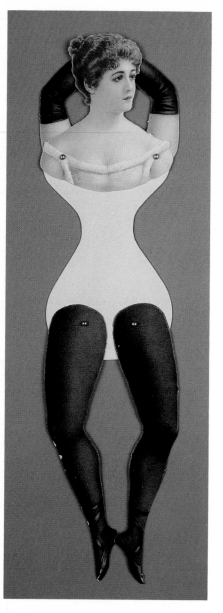

Paper-doll advertisements for Buttermilk Soap, the Chicago *Herald,* and Foster Pianos (*top left*), c. 1895. Designs were freely borrowed by companies throughout the country.

The Dennison Manufacturing Company excelled at dancing dolls, an activated paper doll directly descended from *pantins.* The heads, arms, and legs were made of stiff, glossy pasteboard, and the dolls were about a foot high; c. 1895.

Perhaps the world's most stylish people at the turn of the twentieth century were Alexandra and Edward, Princess and Prince of Wales. These English dolls from about 1900 show the royal couple in their finery; Alexandra's fur-trimmed gown is especially chic.

Royalty continued to fascinate paper-doll manufacturers. These embossed dolls (*left*) are the Princess Royal (Victoria's eldest daughter) and her husband, the crown prince of Germany; England, c. 1900.

Shirley and her family, an impressive handmade paper-doll set from Philadelphia, c. 1904. Shirley boasts many stylish watercolored outfits, including a bridal gown; her babies' clothes and accessories are remarkably fanciful, with no amount of lace or embroidery spared. The artist's great-grandson informed the author that the set was made for a bed-ridden child by a great-aunt.

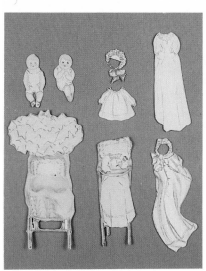

Another handmade set (*facing page*), Connecticut, c. 1905. The figures are unusually individualized and the outfits most elegant; a rather plump lady is an interesting contrast to the dapper young man and woman.

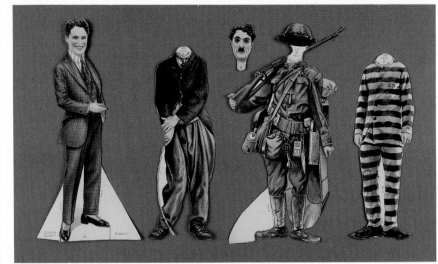

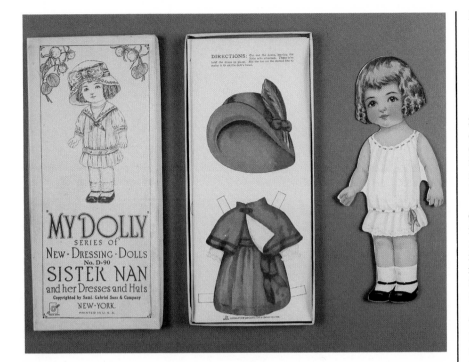

Movies created a new breed of celebrities, and paper dolls took up the theme at once. The dashing Douglas Fairbanks (*facing page, top*) appeared as himself and with costumes from three of his roles. Percy Reeves Movy-Dols, 1920. (*The Macfadden Group, Inc.*).

Similar treatment of another great early movie star, Charlie Chaplin (*facing page, bottom right*). His costume for the Little Tramp includes the fake mustache. Percy Reeves Movy-Dols, 1919. (*The Macfadden Group, Inc.*).

Commercial paper dolls sometimes followed the nineteenth-century tradition of elegance. A good example is "My Dolly"(*left*), a deluxe boxed set issued by Samuel Gabriel Company; Sister Nan is from that series, c. 1908. (*Platt and Munk Company*).

Two of the nattiest 1940s movie stars, Linda Darnell and Tyrone Power, made glamorous paper dolls; note the modesty of Darnell's swimsuit, 1941. (*Merrill Publishing Company*).

Charlie Chaplin *pantin* (*facing page, bottom left*), c. 1919, was made precisely like the *pantins* of prerevolutionary France. The biggest movie star in his most famous costume is forerunner of the immense number of movie-star paper dolls to follow.

Sophisticated Claudette Colbert in a realistic paper-doll guise. The accuracy was achieved by adding color over a black-and-white photograph; 1943. (*Saalfield Publishing Company*).

This exquisitely chromolithographed little-girl doll in her lacy underwear came equipped with a wardrobe that would have been exactly what every little girl in America would have wanted around 1900: a sailor suit for everyday, an afternoon frock, a "Scottish" outfit with matching tam-o'-shanter, a "Sunday best" with beribboned and befeathered bonnet, and, most delightful of all, a fancy-dress shepherdess costume.

The Metropolitan Museum of Art, Gift of Miss Doris V. Reinhard, 41.114 1-9

Elizabeth Taylor (*facing page, top left*) made a ravishing paper doll; Whitman Publishing Company, 1956.

Imaginary celebrities from comic strips, Prince Valiant and Princess Aleta look like the real thing as paper dolls (*facing page, top right*); 1954. (*Saalfield Publishing Company*).

Paper dolls of the past are treasured not only by individual collectors, but by museums as well. This spread from the Spring 1975 *Bulletin of the Metropolitan Museum of Art* (*facing page, bottom*) is a reproduction of an early twentieth-century chromolithographed paper doll from its collection.

Cover and inside pages of Maybelle Mercer's "Dresses Worn by 'First Ladies' of the White House." The dresses are based on the originals in the Smithsonian Institution, and include every first lady up to Eleanor Roosevelt. The four stylized 1930s figures can wear all the gowns, which were of course reproportioned; 1937. (*Saalfield Publishing Company*).

A later version of the First Lady theme used fewer and less detailed gowns and had a generalized 1950s look, but "American Beauty" is a fine costume paper-doll book; 1951. (*Saalfield Publishing Company*).

An *Ankleidepuppen* sheet showing the royal family of Austria, c. 1878. The costumes of the ill-fated Empress Elizabeth, a great beauty of her day, accurately reflect the transition from hoop skirt to bustle.

A treasure for the collector and costume fancier is this McLoughlin bride (*bottom left*), c. 1879; her wardrobe is typical of upper-class women of the period.

Demorest Lady's Magazine was a popular fashion journal of the late nineteenth century, as this cinched-waisted doll from its pages testifies; c. 1895.

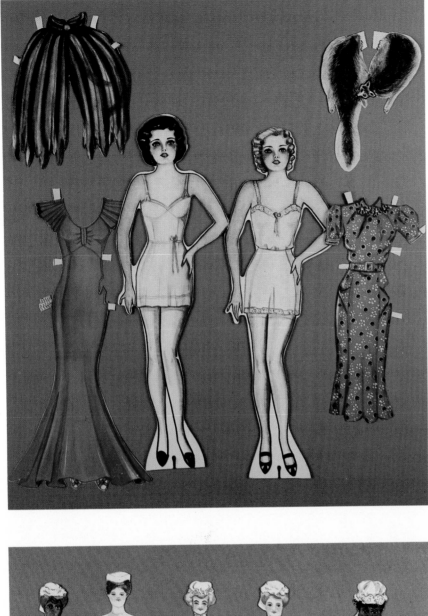

These two cardboard beauties and their extravagant clothes capture the fanciful side of the 1930s—furs, bias-cut dresses, nifty shirtwaists; c. 1935.

Five carefully watercolored handmade paper-doll maids, U.S., c. 1904. Paper dolls faithfully record the changing ideals of family life.

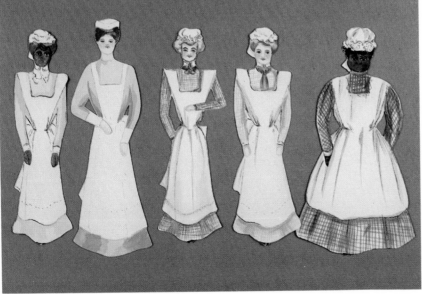

From a large and beautiful Tuck set of English sovereigns, now incomplete, comes Henry III, Edward V, and bad King John; c. 1900.

From a Tuck set of Queen Victoria's large and eminent family, c. 1900: Edward Prince of Wales, Duchess of Edinburgh, Duchess of Connaught, Princess Alice, Victoria Princess Royal, Princess Beatrice, Princess Louisa, Alexandra Princess of Wales, and Princess Helena.

Like all undergarments, corsets were a natural for paper-doll advertisements (*top left*); Bortree Manufacturers, New York, c. 1890.

This stately couple (*top right*), handsomely dressed, may have been packaged with McLaughlin XXXX Coffee, c. 1895; extra clothing was included.

A beautiful paper-doll girl advertising Hood's Sarsparilla, c. 1895. "Plenty of good clothes" are available from the manufacturer to cover the family, whose father wears only a hat and union suit.

A charming paper-doll (*right*) with lovely clothes appropriately advertising Willimantic Thread, c. 1884.

An elaborate and stylish handmade paper doll with fashionable hand-colored clothes and accessories (*bottom left*); U.S., c. 1915.

Jean Goldsmith's paper-doll version of New York man-about-town Richard Karp (*bottom right*). His elaborate accessories include Jane Karp. Felt-tip pen, 1979.

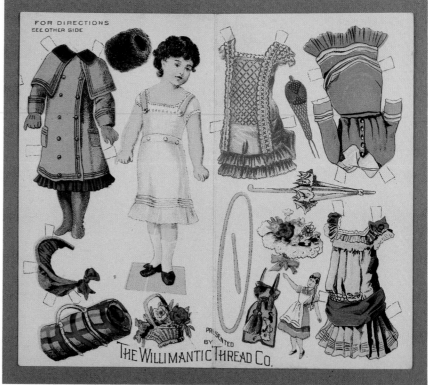

A portrait of the author as a paper doll (*top left*): Oz Garcia's rendition of Anne Tolstoi Wallach, 1979.

Same subject, different artist (*top right*); Jean Goldsmith, 1979. Handmade paper dolls have the advantage of limitless variety of style.

A typical Tuck paper-doll and her wardrobe (*below*), c. 1902. Tuck children have characteristically winsome expressions, brighty colored outfits, and an overall romantic appeal.

Three *pantins* from Germany (*right*); the monkey is particularly grotesque, c. 1890.

Some paper dolls were made to appeal to boys, including paper soldiers. These sheets from Germany (*center*) depict the Austrian army and scenes from the Boer War. J. F. Schrieber, c. 1903.

Rustic scenes were popular paper-doll subjects for German boys. These two (*bottom*) depict cattle breeding and shepherding; Schrieber, c. 1900.

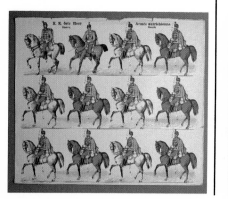

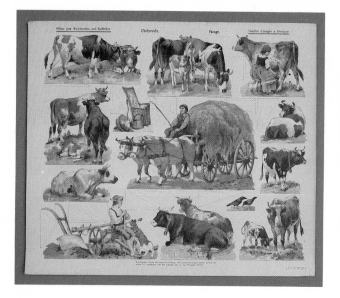

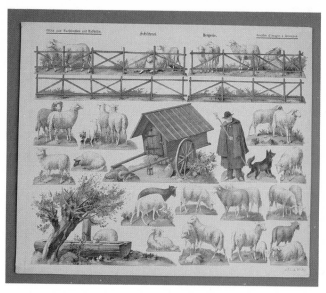

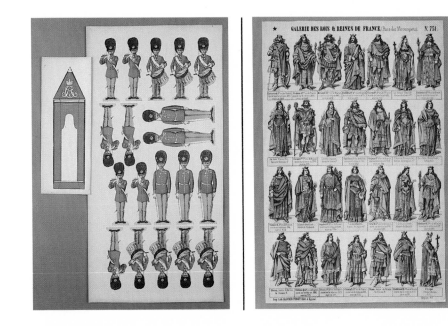

Denmark treasures its paper dolls and makes low-cost reproductions of antique sheets like this one (*top left*), c. 1900, of Danish soldiers.

This colorful "Gallery of Kings and Queens of France" (*top center*), c. 1900, served a similar function to the Tuck sets of British royalty: education through play.

Sheila Young is one of the best-loved paper-doll artists, and the reasons for her enduring appeal are evident in this page from her Lettie Lane series (*top right*); 1909. (*Ladies' Home Journal*).

"The Little Costumer," (*center left*) a charming set from the Pellerin family's celebrated Imagerie d'Epinal, features "varied costumes for both sexes"; c. 1895.

This rabbit's wardrobe (*above*) ranges from elegant evening clothes to tennis and fishing outfits; c. 1910.

These two *pantins* from the Imagerie d'Epinal (*left*), c. 1890, are based on eighteenth-century models of figures from the commedia dell 'arte, Pierrot and Columbine.

Some paper-doll collectors prefer to display those dolls which remind them of family incidents and other real-life episodes. Here are three such examples, from the pages of *McCalls's* magazine: Nosy gives Betsy McCall a bath (1952), Betsy McCall writes from Expo '67 (1967), and Betsy McCall takes a canoe trip (1978). (*The McCall Publishing Company, McCall's*).

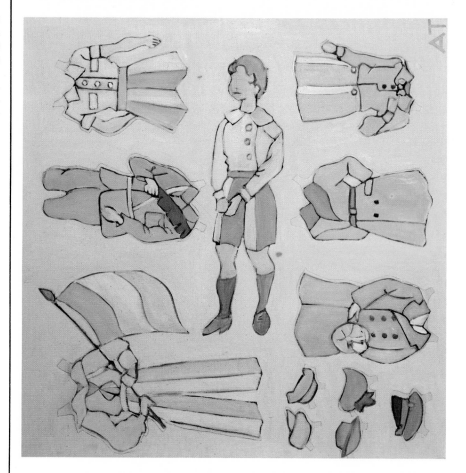

In an interesting reversal, artist Amanda Trager created an oil painting based on paper dolls; 1980.

9

Varieties of Paper Dolls

Once you become aware of paper dolls your first surprise is that so many of them have been made for so long in so many different places. You may want to collect any you can find.

Paper-doll collecting goes quickly. Once your eyes are opened, you will discover finds in friends' houses, antique shops, stationery stores, museum shops. You may even remember some material you yourself have saved from your childhood. And after you understand the scope of paper dolls, you will probably find that some kinds interest you more than others.

Some collectors are enchanted by the prim daintiness of the McLoughlins, however plain their faces. Others search for beautiful fashion dolls with elegant clothes. Some collectors want the embossed and gilded paper dolls of the Victorian and Edwardian periods, or the advertising dolls that tell so much about their times. And today the largest specialty in paper-doll collecting is the celebrity doll, which records the ideal personalities of its time.

Unless your interest is very special indeed, you will probably respond most to one of the main categories.

FASHION PAPER DOLLS

Every paper doll shows changes of clothing. A chronological arrangement of costumes from the two hundred years of paper dolls provides a detailed picture of fashion change.

Paper dolls record a history of underwear, since the dolls frequently begin without outerwear. The early dolls were so detailed and so carefully made that they show a history of underwear fabric as well as color and cut. Miss Lascelles, the watercolor dressmaker's sample of 1798, is obviously dressed in the lawns and muslins of her period. Pastel undergarments are first seen in the McLoughlins of the 1880s. Paper dolls made before World War I wear handmade underclothing, while the 1950s figures show the synthetic underwear of their day. In the most recent paper dolls, underwear becomes less important and even disappears, just as in fashion. Even costume museums do not always offer such a chance for a close look at the history of underwear.

A historical arrangement of paper dolls also gives you a good idea of what the ideal of beauty was in each period. The eighteenth-century ideal of perfect features and carefully-arranged hair gives way to interesting facial expressions and

Rachel Taft Dixon's "Peasant Costumes of Europe" was soundly researched and beautifully authentic; Whitman, 1934. (*Western Publishing Company, Inc.*).

Helen, an American fashion paper doll c. 1910; the details of her costume show the attention paid to fine points.

flowing hair styles in the nineteenth century. The hourglass figure of the nineteenth century changes to the willowy slimness desirable in the twentieth. Even the preferred look for little girls changes through the years. In Shirley Temple's day, every little girl had to have curls and a ladylike look. The tomboy look of the paper-doll children of the 1940s and 1950s is quite different.

Outerwear in paper dolls is always correct for its period. Judge a paper doll against a painting or print, an advertisement or a catalog picture of its time, and you will see the accuracy with which these playthings were designed. Hats, gloves, accessories, parasols, toys, and shoes can all be seen more clearly in paper dolls than in many contemporary sources.

Paper-doll artists were naturally fascinated by clothes, and some of the best artists used paper dolls as costume chronologies. Rachel Taft Dixon's "Historic Costume" is as soundly researched a sequence of several centuries of fashion as any costume book, as is her companion set, "Peasant Costumes of Europe." A beloved paper-doll set of

the 1930s, "Dresses Worn by the 'First Ladies' of the White House" by Maybelle Mercer, shows the gowns of every First Lady from Martha Washington to Eleanor Roosevelt, as they can be seen in the Smithsonian Institution.

There is a special intimacy in cutting out and handling paper costumes that does not exist in print study. Certainly for a child, there are details that stick in the mind as they would from no other source, especially when dolls are large and sturdy. Even uncut, paper dolls seem to impress fashion details in a special way. Perhaps the poses dictated by the need to show clothes head-on, or the fascination of choice of the accessories shown separately, makes the paper doll form so intimate for people who handle them.

With paper dolls you can watch the ideal change from the laced-in waists, mannered posture, and creamy pallor of the nineteenth century to the healthy outdoor athletic look of the late twentieth century. If you want to compare costumes from different periods, paper dolls let you place illustrations from different times side by side. Or if a sin-

gle kind of costume interests you more than others, paper dolls are as revealing as other illustrations, and usually more accessible than books in museums or libraries. A collector can compare hats of different times far more easily than a researcher laboring through costume prints in carefully arranged files.

That favorite theme, costumes of foreign lands, pictured almost since paper dolls began, can make a paper-doll collection on its own. The costumes are usually authentic, and the material ranges from magazine to newspaper supplement, from commercial sets to deluxe boxed editions.

106

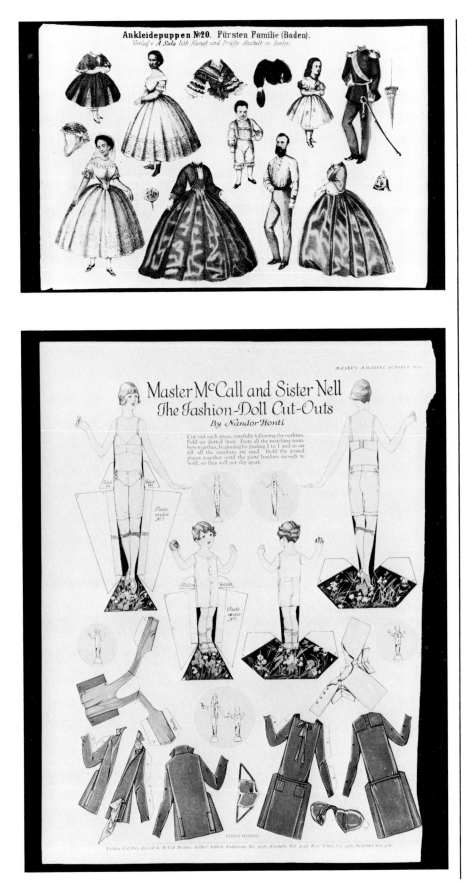

An *Ankleidepuppen* sheet showing the royal family of Baden and their princely outfits; Germany, c. 1880.

Nandor Honti's paper dolls combined art deco fantasy with accuracy in outerwear and underwear. Mrs. McCall's lacy slip and garters are two such telling details (see also next page); 1925. (*McCall's*).

"Magazine Cover Girls" capture the look of "America's prettiest girls" 1940s style; c. 1945. (*Merrill Publishing Company*).

World War II paper uniforms for men and women were accurate in all details; U.S., c. 1943.

108

Standards of beauty change. Malibu Francie reveals the free, swinging California look of the 1970s; Whitman, 1973. (*Mattel, Inc.*).

This embossed paper-doll dancer exemplifies the feminine ideal of its time; U.S., c. 1870.

FAMILY PAPER DOLLS

The family is a child's first social unit, which is why families of paper dolls have been popular from the start. Educational playthings today emphasize doll families for children to learn from and act out fantasies with, usually offering wooden or plastic family members. But in their day, paper families allowed children to add or adapt printed paper dolls easily and cheaply to suit their own tastes. Manufacturers made so many in order to appeal to children of different ages.

The changes through the years in paper-doll families is a collector's interest in itself. The famous magazines series families like Lettie Lane and Betty Bonnet, which were scaled so that all could be played with at once, offered children a huge cast of characters. Imagination could group and regroup endlessly. But paper-doll family groups formed a core that children added to, so that hand-drawn members often can be found with printed ones.

If you decide to collect only families of paper dolls and their servants, you will be gathering a wide range of illustration, printing style, design, fashion, and social history about the American family's activities for two centures. From the maids of a turn-of-the-century family to the automobile culture of 1930s America, paper-doll families offer a nostalgic glimpse of the past.

A deep interest in twins is found throughout paper-doll history. Twins dressed alike in different poses, boy and girl pairs of children, twins dressed in complementary styles, appear consistently. Twins added an extra dimension of fascination for children, and they certainly provided designers an easy reason for multiple figures and dresses. Sometimes, like the paper dolls of Queen Elizabeth's family, a celebrity and a family collection combine to make an interesting specialty for collectors.

The automobile culture took hold in America during the 1930s, and this paper-doll family and their trailer are right in the swing of it; 1938. (*Merrill Publishing Company*). (*facing page*).

"Our Happy Family" shows a dream house and maid, indicating that the 1930s wasn't a Depression for everyone; Gabriel, c. 1938. (*Platt and Munk Company*). (*facing page*).

Variations in paper-doll design were necessary to keep children amused (and buying). This suave paper-doll family is made to walk around their spacious grounds; c. 1934. (*Saalfield Publishing Company*).

From Sheila Young's long-lived Lettie Lane series, the little twin brother and sister. Twins are a recurrent theme in paper-doll history; 1908. (*Ladies' Home Journal*).

Betty Bonnet's father and mother resemble photographs, and their outfits are superbly accurate. Young's realistic treatment was much liked by children; 1916. (*Ladies' Home Journal*).

Celebrity paper dolls include figures in world history: Mary Queen of Scots, Napoleon Bonaparte, Richard the Lion-Hearted, and Robert the Bruce; England, c. 1890.

Albert Einstein, who not only understands his own scientific theories, but can also play the violin and trim a neat mainsheet

Vanity Fair's own paper dolls—no. 6

CELEBRITY PAPER DOLLS

Many collectors specialize only in celebrity paper dolls, and this area has interested researchers more than any other. Groups of celebrities in paper offer a marvelous record of changing interests and popular culture. Some collectors like to gather them from all periods of history, but many others concentrate on movie stars of the great Hollywood years, royal celebrities from the Vic-torian period, or even on fictional celebrities like Elsie Dinsmore and Lewis Carroll's Alice.

Celebrity dolls are the hardest for beginners to find because so many collectors prefer them. Certainly they cost more than other sets. However, they also rise in price faster than other sets, so that they make a sound investment. The only celebrity sets whose prices have not

Alájalov's caricature paper-doll version of Albert Einstein; Vanity Fair, 1934. Einstein's many aspects, represented in paper-doll fashion, include mathematician, violinist, and anti-Nazi warrior. In a satiric comment, the ship's prow is labeled "Adolf" in Yiddish.

A more typical celebrity paper doll is based on lovely movie star Greer Garson; 1944. (*Merrill Publishing Company*).

risen steadily have been political ones like the Nixons, and the more promotional plastic "paper" dolls like those based on television's Kotter. Over time, however, these prices may rise.

The variety of celebrity paper dolls will surprise you, and the chase will challenge you, if you decide to specialize in this group. Collectors in America passionately identify, date, write, and read about their favorites in the paper-doll press, compare paper-doll figures to contemporary paintings, drawings, movie stills, and news photographs. Amateur and professional artists often redraw older celebrity figures and create new versions of them from other illustrative sources. Tom Tierney has been foremost at this, and plans new volumes of theater and ballet stars as well as Presidents and First Ladies in paper-doll form.

Since paper dolls were children's toys, the celebrities of children are perhaps the most endearing. Or, you can collect only pre–World War I celebrities, play guessing games with less familiar figures, or concentrate on male movie stars of the 1940s. However specializd your taste, the material exists.

★ CHARLIE McCARTHY'S RADIO PARTY ★

DIRECTIONS AND RULES FOR PLAYING

1. The game consists of 21 figures . . . one of Charlie McCarthy and four each of Edgar Bergen, Don Ameche, Dorothy Lamour, Nelson Eddy and Robert Armbruster. Also a spinner which determines the play.

2. The game is won by the player who first secures *one* of each of the figures (no duplicates) including Charlie McCarthy, or when a player gets all of the figures (20) without Charlie McCarthy.

3. To start, all figures are arranged in individual groups face up in the center of the table.

4. Players spin. The one getting the highest number starts the game. If two or more persons get the same high number, they spin until tie is broken. Order of play is clockwise from the first player.

5. The game is played by spinning the pointer and following the directions given in the box on which arrow stops. If the arrow stops exactly on the line separating two boxes the player spins again.

6. If a player is unable to complete the play specified, player must pass.

7. Figures taken by a player are placed, face up, in front of him.

8. Each play is completed when player releases figure selected.

9. Pointer must make at least one complete revolution.

10. In making an exchange the player must exchange his figure for a different figure.

11. The figure of Charlie McCarthy is moved only when so specified by pointer.

The Charlie McCarthy Radio Game is fascinating and requires a certain amount of skill in playing. While the object is to secure a full set of figures, a player should constantly maneuver his plays so that he will prevent his opponents securing a complete set.

Copyright by Standard Brands Incorporated

CHARLIE McCARTHY

EDGAR BERGEN

NELSON EDDY

ROBERT ARMBRUSTER

DON AMECHE

DOROTHY LAMOUR

Linda Darnell Paper Dolls
Authorized Edition

Standard Brands, the sponsor of Edgar Bergen's radio program, issued these paper dolls as part of an advertising campaign in 1938. The figures represent Charlie McCarthy (the dummy), Bergen, Nelson Eddy, Robert Armbruster, Don Ameche, and Dorothy Lamour. (*Standard Brands, Inc.*).

Queen Holden's paper-doll version of a fresh-faced Judy Garland. The set came with a gigantic wardrobe; Whitman, 1941.

Authorized edition of the stunning Linda Darnell, sumptuously gowned; 1953. (*Saalfield Publishing Company*).

Direct from Lawrence Welk's popular television show come the Lennon Sisters, with 104 costumes and accessories; Whitman, 1958. (*Telekew Productions*).

A sampling of the vast variety of celebrity paper dolls. The notables include Eleanor Roosevelt, George and Martha Washington, Queen Isabella (with Columbus), Albert Einstein, and Charlie Chaplin; 1925–1980. (*Cardesign*).

The toast of Broadway, Mary Martin as a lively paper doll; 1944. (*Saalfield Publishing Company*).

Celebrity children made especially appropriate and appealing paper dolls. Caroline Kennedy is shown as a petite horsewoman; Magic Wand, c. 1962.

Among the many paper-doll incarnations of Shirley Temple is this large cardboard model, a promotional giveaway; c. 1935.

Geraldine Farrar, the most popular American opera singer of her time, with costumes from two of her most celebrated roles, Madame Butterfly and Carmen; Percy Reeves Movy-Dols, 1920.

The popular comic-strip heroine Blondie appeared as a paper doll with her family, the Bumsteads; Whitman, 1948. (*King Features*).

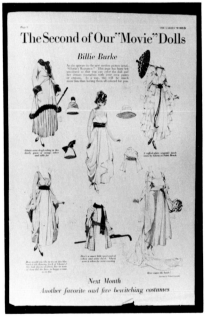

Emilie, one of the Dionne quintuplets, plays house; Whitman, 1936. The Dionne girls fascinated the public in the 1930s. Note the slotted stove and tabbed food and utensils.

An imposing paper George Washington, quite lifelike, especially around the eyes; M.C. & K., c. 1895.

Kaiser Wilhelm II of Germany, looking imperious even in paper; Germany, c. 1895.

A popular vaudeville and movie star and wife of producer Flo Ziegfeld, Billie Burke as a fetching paper doll in her pre–*Wizard of Oz* days; *Ladies' World,* 1916. The gown at top left is a "ruffled white organdy frock worn at Palm Beach."

ADVERTISING PAPER DOLLS

Paper dolls were selling products almost as soon as they could be produced in volume. Small and flat, they could be tucked into products, sent through the mails, or included on packaging. Fashion dolls were used as advertisements for dressmakers, actresses, and dancers.

What is most often meant by an advertising paper doll is one which carries a manufacturer's message. Some were mail-ordered, others were included in packages of coffee or flour or on packages of bread or cereal. No one is quite certain what makes a complete set, when exactly the dolls were published, or how many for each product were printed. Beginners can find completely unknown advertising paper dolls and contribute to the body of in-

formation quite as well as experts.

From the turn of the century through the 1930s these dolls were numerous. The names and slogans found on them, particularly on the backs along with advertising copy, are some of the most famous brand names in American history. Today many giant companies like the Coca-Cola Company, which issued many kinds of premiums for many years, are realizing what treasures these articles are, and are making a corporate effort to collect them. Their prices now exceed the original costs by many thousands of dollars.

A collector learns quickly that few big companies have preserved old advertising, or outdated paper premiums. Still fewer smaller enterprises, like department stores, have

had the space to save advertising for more than a few recent years. A great deal of paper material has been discarded to make room for new things. However, not all of it was destroyed, and the advertising paper dolls are perhaps easiest for beginners to find.

They continue even today, as paper dolls grow to be more an adult convention than a child's toy notion. Save current examples whenever you see them. They quickly turn up on dealers' lists for one or two dollars, and in a year are worth considerably more. Specializing in advertising paper dolls is an amusing and instructive pastime, and a real challenge for anyone who wants to add to the fund of paper-doll information.

118

Behr-Manning, maker of Barney's Sandpaper, used their bear symbol in a paper-doll advertisement; c. 1913. (*facing page, left*).

Grace, a large paper-doll advertisement for Dr. Miles' Laxative Tablets; c. 1912. (*facing page, right*).

These exotically costumed paper children advertised an unidentified product; U.S., c. 1880.

This sweet paper doll opens to proclaim the virtues of Buttermilk Toilet Soap, "the best soap in the world." A set of sixteen dolls was available by mail from the manufacturer; Canada, c. 1885.

A movable paper doll wearing leotards, accurately reflecting (and advertising) the fashions of her day; c. 1961. (*Determined Productions, Inc.*).

A modern version of the paper doll as underwear advertisement features Eiderlon panties; Textiles Inc., 1978. (*Spun-Lo Eiderlon, A Division of Ti-Caro*).

Another of Maidenform's "I dreamed I was cut out for fun" brassiere ads; 1961.

"Woman's Place is in the Ford" reads this ad; modern woman's many roles are suitably suggested in paper-doll style; 1949. (*Ford Motor Company*).

Paper dolls can serve an editorial function, as in this illustration for an article on buying children's clothes; 1980. (*Working Mother Magazine A.D.: Nina Scerbo*).

BUYING CLOTHES FOR CHILDREN AND OTHER HEADACHES

BY HESTER MUNDIS

Buying clothes for children is one of those insane ordeals many people are subjected to at one time or another. Mothers are particularly vulnerable, though fathers, aunts, uncles and grandparents are not immune. Even the casual gift-giver has been known to hit the aspirin bottle because of it. It is a task that challenges the rules of order by which our universe functions.

It all begins when the baby is born—sometimes before—with a quaint initiation ritual. This exercise in basic migraines is known as Buying the Layette. For the unwary, the experience can be traumatic. To protect yourself from befuddlement and self-doubt, you must recognize one essential fact: Children's clothing sizes are the invention of a deranged manufacturers' cartel. Once you accept this, things become easier.

Inside each article of infant's clothing is a little tag—not unlike those the law forbids you to remove from sofas, pillows and reclining chairs—ostensibly designed to guide you in proper fitting. Since babies don't have hip, bust, waist or shoulder measurements to speak of, manufacturers, in obvious desperation, have sized their goods in terms of a baby's age, weight and sometimes height. They might just as well have provided guidelines based on eye color.

Their Newborn label is a fair example. Reason dictates that Newborn is the size you'd want for baby's first months. But reason, you have to keep in mind, has no part in the buying of children's clothes. This becomes evident when you discover that each manufacturer has very definite and different ideas about how long and fat your newborn should be.

If your baby is a hefty 10-pounder, the child will be out of luck when it comes to getting clothes. Too big for the Newborn size, too short for the next, he or she will be relegated to the floppy-footed, slack-sleeved look one associates with performing animals and cute actresses dressed in men's striped pajamas. Salespeople seem to favor this look; I have yet to meet one who recommends buying clothing that actually fits a child. Since birth, my kids have dressed six months to two years ahead of their time.

Buying infants' clothing sets the irrational tone for the whole headache-causing endeavor that follows. Baby clothes run from Newborn to 24 Months. When the child reaches the age of two years (approximately 36 to 38 inches, 33 to 36 pounds, according to manufacturers' descriptions), he or she—ready or not—enters a brand-new sizing bracket called Toddler.

Toddler sizes run from 2T to 4T. Now you might reason that a 24 Months size should be the same as a 2T. But, as I said, when buying kids' clothing, reason has to be kept at bay: 2T is bigger than 24 Months. The sizes are not only unidentical, but often can't be found in the same department. I have a friend with twin three-year-old daughters. Because one child is smaller, my friend has to shop for their clothes on different floors. And this is only the beginning of the bizarre division of children's clothes. To be forewarned helps, but not much.

There is a 4 to 6X category for girls and a 4 to 7 category for boys. (I have no idea why girls have the X and boys don't. I suppose it has something to do with chromosomes.) Then comes the 7 to 14 range for girls and the 8 to 14 grouping for boys. After that, the 3 to 13 Juniors for girls and the 12 to 20 Students for boys.

Though the numbers seem as though they correspond to the child's age, they have virtually nothing to do with it. Your six-year-old daughter might wear a size 8 while her 12-year-old sister wears a size 5. And to make things really confusing, the 12-year-old can save her size 4 for the six-year-old to grow into! Even

110   WORKING MOTHER, MARCH 1980

MAGAZINE PAPER DOLLS

One of the easiest and least expensive kinds of paper dolls to collect are magazine sheets. You can often find them intact in their magazine for two or three dollars. If you are willing to fuss with cut dolls—which means collecting bits and pieces to complete a set—you can have them for a minimum of money.

These dolls were so common in the 1920s and 1930s, so much a part of every editor's plan for women's magazines, that they exist in great number, so there are plenty for you to find. Many collectors began by leafing through old magazines in back-issue stores, thrift shops, even junk piles. These throwaway pages hold some of the best samples of illustration in the paper-doll world. Mail-order lists always have magazine sheets for sale; they are an easy and available group of paper dolls for any beginner.

Today's magazines sometimes use the paper-doll concept editorially. Examples appear every month, as a new generation of art directors rediscovers the idea and finds it use-

121

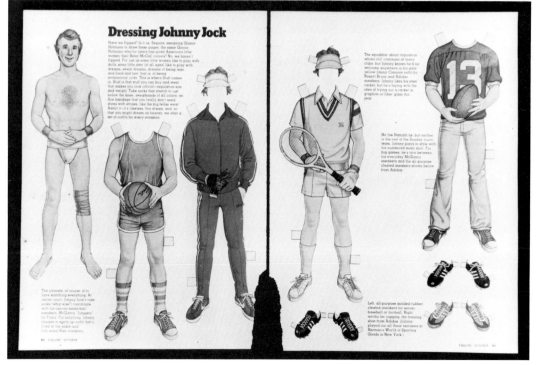

Sheila Young's Betty Bonnet series can be obtained complete by the diligent collector. Betty's college cousins would enhance anyone's set; 1917. (*Ladies' Home Journal*).

Kewpies were favorites in all forms, including paper dolls. These angelic-faced examples are accompanied by quaint little stories; *Woman's Home Companion*, 1913.

Ginnie Hofmann, creator of Betsy McCall, drew Johnny Jock for an article in *Esquire* magazine, c. 1976. (Esquire Publishing Inc.)

Paper dolls have limitless appeal to nostalgia buffs. Corwin Knapp Linson's "On Furlough in France" from his World War I series is no exception; 1918. *Delineator, (Butterick Fashion Marketing Company)*.

Sheila Young drew the Polly Pratt series for *Good Housekeeping*, but her excellent artwork, like this sweet-faced country cousin, was compromised by low-contrast color printing; 1920. (*Good Housekeeping*).

ful. Remember to clip these when you see them; they show up a few months after issue date on dealers' lists, always costing more than the magazine, even a recent one.

The older magazine paper dolls, like the Sheila Young pages, are the easiest sets to obtain complete from dealers. The prices keep rising, but if you keep a list of what you need to finish a set you will always be ready to pounce on a bargain. All of them are charming, attractive, and interesting.

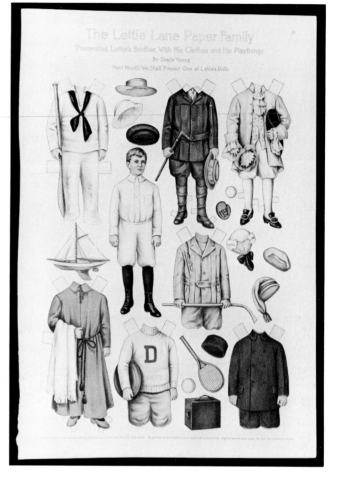

A beautiful bride from the Betty Bonnet series. Among the lavish costumes is a Red Cross uniform; 1918. (*Ladies' Home Journal*).

This well-dressed little chap is from Young's first series, Lettie Lane; 1909. (*Ladies' Home Journal*).

Vintage Young, from the time of America's entry into World War I: Betty Bonnet's army and navy cousins; 1917. (*Ladies' Home Journal*).

NEWSPAPER PAPER DOLLS

Paper dolls of newsprint are the most fragile of all, and represent a special challenge many collectors enjoy. Crudely printed and often very small, they offer handling problems and preservation difficulties. Nevertheless, they provide the same record of their day as more expensive and sturdier paper dolls.

Newspaper dolls have a special pop look, probably because they were always the most up-to-the-minute designs and ideas. They were also free for most children,

handed over by parents. Sometimes you can find them with extra home-made dresses for the little figures. They are all reasonably priced, available, and can often be found in big lots from dealers who want to dispose of the flimsy squares before they disintegrate. And even within so small a category of paper dolls as newspaper figures, artists kept the ideas varied.

Comic-strip paper dolls have a long history of their own. Anna Belle was one of the earliest, drawn

by F. Gere from 1913 to 1916. In the 1930s, Winnie Winkle glorified the career girl, and her creator, Martin Branner, dressed her in the latest

Although crudely printed and fragile, newspaper paper dolls capture the past with a charm uniquely their own. Samples from the 1930s and 1940s include Tillie the Toiler, Newspaper Dolly, Mr. Willie Waddle, and Jane Arden. Many of the costumes and accessories were submitted by readers.

glamor fashions. Jane Arden's artist, Monte Barrett, liked to vary the traditional standing dolls with seated figures, three-quarter views, and profiles, which tested the ability of readers who sent in designs. The idea of using reader's designs was carried on in Tillie the Toiler, Flying Jennie, Dixie Dugan, and Brenda Starr in the 1940s and 1950s. Paul Robertson drew Etta Kett; Chic Young, Blondie; Jimmy Murphy, Toots and Caspar; V.F. Hamlin, Alley Oop.

In the late 1940s, the monthly comic books took over some comic-strip paper dolls. Bill Woggon's famous Katy Keene progressed to a comic book of her own. Several characters from the comics, including Blondie, L'il Abner, and Tillie the Toiler became commercial paper-doll booklets because they had become so popular through their original newspaper exposure.

Flash Gordon was one of the most beautifully drawn newspaper dolls, and the set is prized by col-

lectors. But as paper-doll prices keep going up, nearly every newspaper doll is growing more valuable. Look for Flapper Fanny from the mid-twenties, Dan Rudolph's designs from the same period with titles like "Stella Steps Out in Rompers and Bloomers," and of course the most famous of all, Little Orphan Annie, who began her career in comic strips and is the heroine of ten major paper-doll sets, including a 1968 Colorforms plastic version.

HANDMADE PAPER DOLLS

According to many collectors, the most delightful of all paper dolls are the handmade examples from all periods. They are the most individual, and often the most carefully designed. Even though amateur artists did the bulk of them, they are often accurate and genuine pictures of their times. The earliest ones, dating from the days when women were given drawing and watercolor lessons as a basic part of their education, are especially pleasing. Later paper-dolls were cruder, sketched by little girls and dressed in paper samples from catalogs and magazines. All are worth preserving and collecting.

Handmades turn up in the most unexpected places of all, because it is hard for dealers to catalog them. To find them you must develop an eye for the insides of old packages, as well as the habit of poking into old

magazines, Bibles, and sewing boxes, children's storage places in days past. A box of old envelopes and postcards at a country fair yielded the finest handmade family in my collection.

Sometimes you will discover a complete handmade set. You can also find handmade additions to popular printed dolls, especially the Boston *Herald* Ladies and the Sheila Young dolls, which seemed to inspire amateurs. Since these handmades were the cheapest of paper playthings, many of them were made over two hundred years age.

The range of subject is as great among handmades as it is in any other paper-doll category. Printed dolls are often found with handmade additions to their wardrobes, beautifully drawn and colored in the style of the period. Every handmade is cut out of its time in history.

Jean Goldsmith's secretary paper doll has clothing only for her upper half. As with most secretaries, the rest is hidden by a desk; 1980.

Every paper doll mirrors its time. This embossed paper doll has contemporary handmade costumes; U.S., c. 1885.

TUCK PAPER DOLLS

The work of Raphael Tuck & Sons is so fine and so special in its romantic appeal that many collectors specialize in it, and almost all collectors value it highly.

Adult Tuck dolls all have similar expressions and lavishly beautiful clothing. Tuck children also share a common expression, doll-like and wide-eyed, and come with fanciful

and beautifully colored costumes.

Most Tucks are carefully marked on the backs with their titles and the number of the sets in which they were printed. This makes it easy to

gather complete sets, or to know if you need a matching hat or another costume. Most Tucks came in heavy cardboard folders, themselves treasures of decoration; these folders are needed to make up a really complete set. All the Tuck material presents a picture of a gentler era: ordered, pretty, and innocent.

PAPER DOLLS FROM OTHER COUNTRIES

One of the easiest ways to begin collecting paper dolls is to look for the modern material still being printed in Europe and Japan. Naturally, these dolls are inexpensive because they are still being sold as children's toys in shops with other inexpensive games and amusements. If you or your friends travel, you can quickly pick up contemporary paper-doll sets for very little, pack them easily in the smallest suitcase, and gather a paper-doll collection which will increase in value almost immediately. You will also have the challenge of discovering how paper dolls differ from place to place, and how each seems to fit its own cultural background.

Though plastic has taken over the place of paper toys in America and England, paper dolls are common in less industrialized countries. Even if you collect them only as travel souvenirs, you can amass an interesting group that will quickly fill an album.

Antique and print shops, and even book shops, in Europe are sources for older foreign paper dolls. Although relatively inexpensive compared to most antique objects, the oldest ones may cost more than you want to pay, unless you have a lucky find. Again, you must be demanding. Almost no print or book dealer will remember, when you first ask, that he has a paper-doll or two tucked away, but paper dolls can often be found in narrow print drawers marked "Miscellaneous" or among children's books. The market has been small up until now, and the material difficult to categorize or even date. If you know what you are looking at, even a

stray costume or hat will mean something to you, and can often be had for almost no money.

Germany produced marvelous paper dolls and toys almost from the beginning of paper-doll history, and though much of the material has been destroyed, there is still a great deal to be found. German paper dolls were often treated like precious objects, especially the beautiful embossed ones.

Germany and Austria were famous for paper soldiers meant for boys, as a substitute for more costly lead soldiers. Paper soldiers are as old as paper dolls; the fascination, unlike an individual doll figure, is for multiples so that regiments can be formed.

Jonathan Newman, who, with his wife, Barbara, has a shop in Clifton Park, New York called The Paper Soldier, has written many articles on the history of paper soldiers. He reports that Louis XIV commissioned an elaborate set for his son in 1670. German and French printers created thousands of sheets of soldiers over the next two centuries. A Strasbourg printer, Seyfried, celebrated the armies of Louis XV on paper. By the late eighteenth century, when paper toys began to appear

Pantins from Germany, c. 1885, exhibit a predilection for grotesque faces and bodies.

128

all over Europe, Jean Frederick Striedbeck produced cardboard soldiers in Strasbourg. These early sheets are a superb source for military historians, just as paper dolls record useful details for costume researchers.

The Pellerins issued paper soldiers in the nineteenth century, many with lithography by Charles Pinot, who later formed his own printing establishment, Pinot et Sagaire. By 1890 Germany was printing paper soldiers in great number; J. F. Schrieber in Esslingen and Hoeinstein and Lang in Berlin were among the leading printers. Soldiers printed by Silbermann and Fischbach, were early recognized as valuable works of art, and today are priced high. Boys cut them out and mounted them on woodblocks to make them stand, creating their own paper armies. Newman believes, sensibly, that World War I put an end to the widespread interest in paper soldiers for children.

Pantin, Germany, date unknown.

This sheet of paper dolls from Germany is full of detailed illustration; c. 1845.

Dolly, a German paper doll made for export to English-speaking countries, date unknown. She is sewn into an attractive card to create the illusion of a little girl at a window when the card is closed; her wardrobe is inside.

Denmark today has a lively interest in paper toys, old and new. Sentries in full regalia still guard the palace in Copenhagen, and paper versions of them are still sold for children. The National Museum shop sells beautiful low-cost reproductions of its collection, and print shops in Copenhagen offer many antique sheets similar to those in the museums, as well as good collections of Austrian and German sheets of the nineteenth century.

Sweden, Finland, and Norway also sell modern paper dolls. Evidently Scandinavian children, whose mothers embroider so beautifully, are still encouraged to learn sewing and cutting by playing with detailed paper dolls.

Greek children still cut out paper toys at Christmas to decorate holiday rooms. Italian girls buy paper dolls in the Barbie mode, sleek contemporary girls with hip wardrobes; ask for *cartoni da ritagliare*. In the Soviet Union the paper dolls are copies of Italian designs overlaid with Cyrillic script; it seems a pity that the Russians do not copy better material. Paper animals seem to be favorites for Russian children.

Japan sells paper-doll families in toy stores. Mexican children have most of the American Disney and toy-related paper dolls, but at prices that make them toys of the upper classes. Native Mexican costumes are also attractively recreated in paper (compare them to American versions of Mexican costume). Spain prints paper dolls cheaply for children, some with plastic scissors included in the packing.

France, birthplace of the paper doll, has a long history of paper dolls designed around provincial costumes, royalty, families, children, fashion, and furniture. In the nineteenth century, France produced many soldiers, panoramas, peep shows, toy paper theaters, and other amusements of the same kind.

Sets are still to be found in Paris antique shops and in print shops that specialize in children's books and teaching tools of an earlier time. Paper miniature furniture, another special interest for many collectors, was a particular favorite of French publishers well up to the beginning of the present century.

France, which produced the Pellerins, famous for centuries for their colorful prints and paper amusements, is the home of the fashion doll and the soldier. France is today reprinting some old paper dolls, and shopkeepers say that children are buying them as readily as adults.

Collectors get a special joy from traveling in countries where paper dolls are still sold for today's children.

These cardboard soldiers make warlike paper toys; U.S., c. 1910.

Danish modern in paper dolls: a recognizably contemporary family and their somewhat hippy clothes; UniSet, Denmark, 1976.

Bunad, a paper doll with regional Norwegian costumes; c. 1955.

Little brother and big sister are attractive paper dolls from Sweden; Frisk & Ralf, Stockholm, 1978.

Minna and Mika, rather serious-looking paper dolls from Finland. Their outfits are folk inspired; Star-Pap Oy, Finland, date unknown.

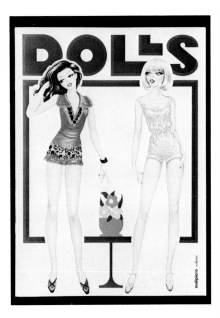

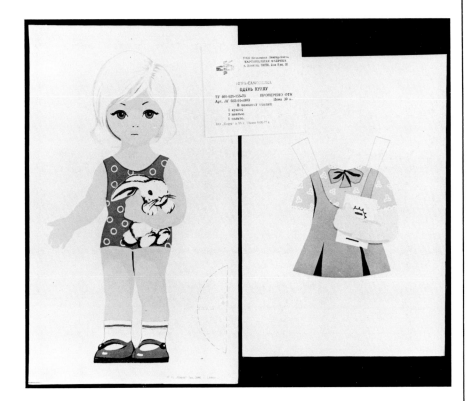

These Greek cutouts feature native costumes and customs; c. 1970.

Two unusually glamorous paper dolls from Italy; Malpiero, 1975.

Anna, another chic Italian *ritagliare* ("recut"); Auguri di Mondadori, c. 1975.

This large-eyed Russian paper doll is apparently a copy of an Italian model; USSR, date unknown.

Another cutout from the Soviet Union features animals from the National Zoo; date unknown.

Paper-doll family from Japan and a room from their rather Westernized home; c. 1965.

These Mexican paper dolls wear costumes as beautiful as they are authentic; Mexico City, 1964.

An American version of Mexico makes an interesting contrast with the real article. Rosetta's eyes move from side to side when the doll is moved, and her costume is claimed to be "authentic"; Magic Doll, date unknown.

BB of Spain comes with a complete wardrobe for all seasons; Barcelona, c. 1965.

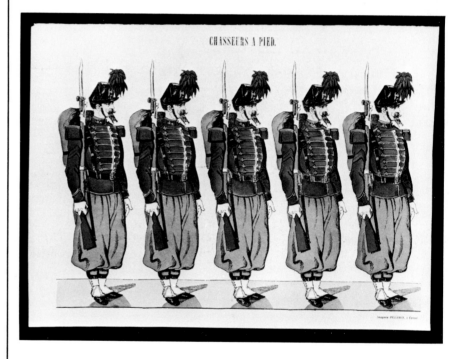

These stylish French paper dolls depict Russian costumes; *La poupee modèle,* 1899. The small and intricate figures are printed on very flimsy paper.

Foot soldiers from Pellerin's Imagerie d'Epinal; c. 1890.

136

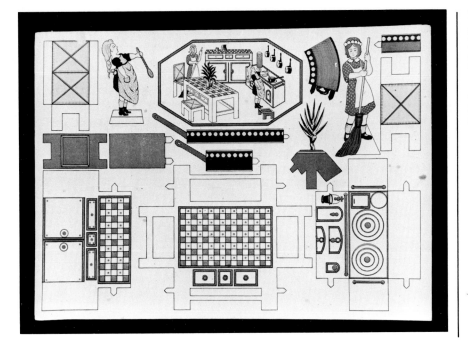

Décorama, "a revolution in the art of decoupage," illustrating Little Red Riding Hood. Paper furniture has always attracted collectors; Editions Volumetrix, France, date unknown.

An earlier version of French miniature paper furniture with a distinctive art deco look; c. 1925.

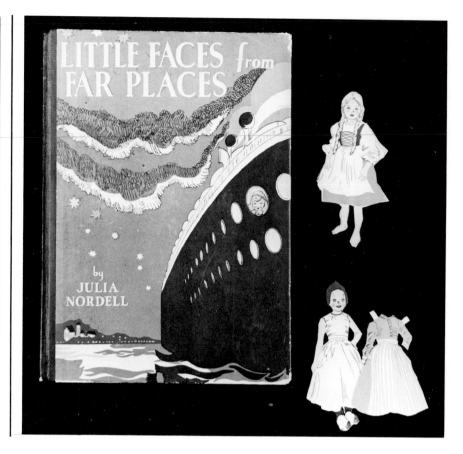

Jacki is an adorable paper-doll child with charming outfits and paper animals; Editions Jelp, France, c. 1925.

"Little Faces from Far Places" sums up the appeal of paper dolls from foreign lands; Grosset & Dunlap, 1933. (*Platt and Munk Company*).

HOUSES AND THEATERS OF PAPER

Though not strictly in the scope of paper-doll collecting, the many examples of paper houses and furniture, as well as the marvelous paper theaters of the nineteenth century, usually fascinate collectors.

Paper houses have been made by almost all the famous publishers, and some are being reprinted as curiosities for today's children. "Dolly's Mansion" from 1890, McLoughlin's folding doll houses, and Tuck's 1909 "Picture-Building Doll House" are some early ones. "Dolly Blossom's Bungalow" of 1917, Whitman's "Let's Play House" of 1932, many advertising rooms and houses from Buttermilk Toilet Soap, and Maple Flake Products, Pillsbury's, and New England Mince Meat were favorite paper playthings of the past.

Paper theaters form an enormous category of interest. Born with the panoramas, peep shows, and paper trick amusements of the early nineteenth century, theaters were often cut and put together by boys while their sisters played with paper dolls. Robert Louis Stevenson's well-known 1884 essay on them, "Penny Plain and Two-Pence Coloured," describes the Skelt paper theaters he enjoyed as a child, and which no less a critic than Max Beerbohm believed a strong influence on Stevenson's writing. Germany had Kasperl theaters of great beauty and intricacy, and England had Pollock theaters, which came with scripts and paper figures of famous actors of the day so a child could replay the drama at home.

Both paper houses and theaters (and pop-up books, like those of Lothar Meggendorfer) in their original state are quite costly, and usually out of bounds for the average collector. Many originals are in museums. As they are being reissued in replica, however, they make interesting reference material as a related interest for anyone fascinated by paper dolls.

10

Building Your Collection

HOW TO START A PAPER-DOLL COLLECTION

Collecting is a highly individual activity, and your idea of a complete collection is as good as anybody's. There are no rights and wrongs in paper dolls. The Queen Holden baby you like is as important as the McLoughlin you find ugly. The more you know, the better your collection will be, but it can always display your personal taste. If you want to collect teddy bears with cute clothes, fine. If pre-1900 fashion enchants you, fine, too. Most people are glad to find any paper doll, at first; then likes and dislikes surface quickly.

You can arrange a chronological group, as the illustrations are arranged in this book. You can specialize in advertising dolls, or celebrity faces, or your own childhood paper dolls. But the standard categories are only a start. You can choose a century or even a decade. You can collect only paper dolls in mint condition, or only cut material. You can forget catalogs, chronologies, and references and collect just what you like with no system at all. You can collect a set of just one artist's work.

For example, Queen Holden's designs are notable for their originality, clever ideas, and gentle illustration. A checklist of all her work shows more than sixty sets, many of them large and elaborate. Holden herself is not sure how many sets she designed. But each has an idea of its own, usually a different one from any she, or any other artist, has used before. Holden babies and children are easy to recognize by their large size, big eyes, sweet expression, and rounded bodies. Holden babies had many accessories, like nursery furniture, lotion bottles, cotton jars, dolls, toy animals, and baby buntings. (Only as a paper-doll collector did I realize how completely my notion of a proper baby layette was based on the Holden paper dolls I owned as a child.)

Holden adults are models of their period, their outfits straight from fashion magazines of their day, their cigarettes, aprons, and hats a record of their times. The covers of the books are usually interesting, and the titles frequently reflect Depression values. Holden used dolls with eyes that moved, dolls with hairdos that could be varied, dolls that appeared to walk. Her celebrity sets have a special charm. Prices for all her sets are high, and they rise steeply year by year.

Sheila Young is another enduring favorite, and an equally prolific paper doll designer. Her pretty Lettie Lane and Betty Bonnet families were favorites for millions of American children, as was her later Polly Pratt series. Young's study of fine arts shows in the pastel coloring, attention to costume detail, and the realism of her characters. The idea of matched size dolls enabling a child to assemble a huge group, was copied by many artists. Her tiny extras, especially her paper-doll dolls complete with cloth-

The aptly named Queen Holden was queen of the paper-doll world. These pages of baby and accessories show her fascinating command of detail, including the tiny bottles of boric acid and olive oil and the elaborate carriage and bassinet; Whitman, 1931. (*Western Publishing Company, Inc.*).

Holden's Sleeping Dolls had punch-out eyes that blinked; all her paper-doll children had large eyes, sweet expressions, and rounded bodies; Whitman, 1945. (*Western Publishing Company, Inc.*).

A Holden sampler: All Size Dolls show that an androgynous sweetness prevails in all ages; Whitman, 1945. (*Western Publishing Company Inc.*).

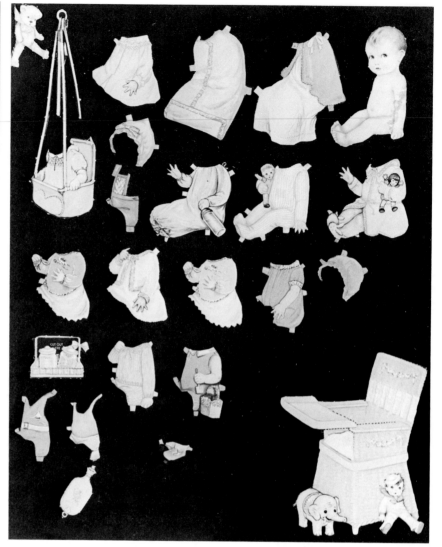

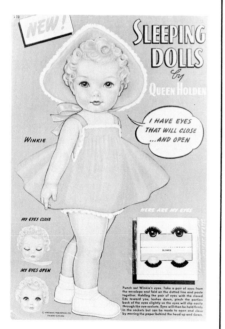

Baby Ann came nude, but Holden supplied plenty of clothes and nursery furniture; Whitman, 1933. (*Western Publishing Company, Inc.*).

Holden's covers were always interesting, as is this one featuring Patsy Ann and her trunkful of clothes; Whitman, 1939. (*Western Publishing Company, Inc.*).

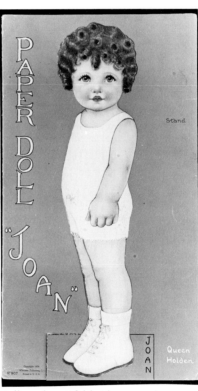

This early Holden paper doll has Baby Brother and his pet teddy bear, with sixty pieces to cut out; Whitman, 1929. (*Western Publishing Company, Inc.*).

Sally, a beautiful bride somewhere between childhood and adulthood. Her huge eyes are a Holden trademark; Whitman, 1950. (*Western Publishing Company, Inc.*).

Joan's enormous eyes, pursed lips, and curly hair suggest that Holden may have been inspired by the young Joan Crawford; Whitman, 1928. (*Western Publishing Company, Inc.*).

141

Holden's adults were sophisticated versions of her basic model. This glamor girl boasts twenty different hairdos; Whitman, 1941. (*Western Publishing Company, Inc.*).

A most darling Darlikin Doll epitomizes Holden's enduring appeal; Whitman, 1938. (*Western Publishing Company, Inc.*).

ing, are particularly valued by collectors. As a whole her work forms a fascinating record of the years between 1908 and 1921, with all the toys, cameras, favored dog and cat breeds, clothing, customs, and playthings of those years.

Bill and Corinne Bailey worked for the Saalfield Company in the 1930s. They designed many celebrity dolls, including all of the Shirley Temple bestsellers of the 1930s and 1940s. The Baileys were the first paper-doll artists to use photography as the basis for their work, adding tints in layers to black-and-white photographs of movie stars for a specially realistic look. Their style, based on realism and contemporary fashion, is easy to recognize after short study.

Rachel Taft Dixon studied costume design and illustration, graduating from Pratt Institute in 1914. A children's-book designer, she moved naturally to paper dolls. The idea for both "Historic Costume" and "Peasant Costume" were her own, and each costume was carefully researched and painstakingly drawn. Each figure and each article

of clothing is a small gem, especially when you compare them to more slapdash designs in contemporary sets. Her characters from *Little Women* and *The Five Little Peppers*

Bill and Corinne Bailey specialized in celebrity paper dolls, using black-and-white photographs as a basis and adding tints in layers. Their skill is clear in this set of the exotic Hedy Lamarr; 1942. (*Merrill Publishing Company*).

Rachel Taft Dixon combined talent and scholarly research to create costume paper dolls from different eras and lands. Her accuracy made dolls like Annie Laurie (1700 A.D.) truly educational; Lowe, 1941. (*Samuel Lowe Company, Inc.*).

Betty Campbell's work excels in an abundance of realistic detail. Her "Nurse and Doctor" paper dolls are most lifelike, the doctor having been based on a real physician, Robert Baird; 1952. (*Saalfield Publishing Company*).

are as beautiful as any children's-book illustration, while her kittens, pigs, dogs, and bears are fascinating in their link to her human figures, sharing the same expressive eyes and natural poses.

Orpha Klinker studied art in California and Paris. Best known for her portraits in oil and pastel and for historical scenes on china, she was an associate fellow of the American Institute of Fine Arts. Her contribution to paper dolls is the curious Betty Bobbs, which featured highly original and amusing drawings with wigs, clever accessories, and startling color. Klinker dolls are not favorites among collectors who favor the cute and pretty, but they are a high point in originality.

Betty Campbell, another prolific artist, created more than fifty sets between the 1930s and 1960s. Starting with "Costume Party" in 1930, she used separate faces for the costume changes and designed a beautiful box and a story booklet. She went on to produce roundabout dolls which had a three-dimensional appeal, sewing-book sets in which scissors, crayons, embroidery thread, and needles could be used to dress heavy wood figures, the Williamsburg Restoration paper-doll set with its authentic costume design, and a great many celebrity favorites, including Linda Darnell, Arlene Dahl, Barbara Britton, and Juliet Jones. Campbell's insistence on realistic detail gives her work a recognizable quality and interest.

Grace Drayton, the creator of Dolly Dingle, is a famous paper-doll artist who is easy for beginners to recognize. Her Campbell Soup-kid's look can be seen in the expressions of puppies, kittens, dolls, and adult faces as well as in her children. Between 1913 and 1933 her unique output appeared in real dolls, on china, in jewelry, in bestselling prints, and much more. Her poses, ideas, and clever subject matter were little masterpieces of the paper-doll world. Her older sister, Margaret G. Hays, who began her career writing a 1906 comic strip for a Philadelphia newspaper, is known best for her "Fairy Tale Favorites," also in a style unique to the artist.

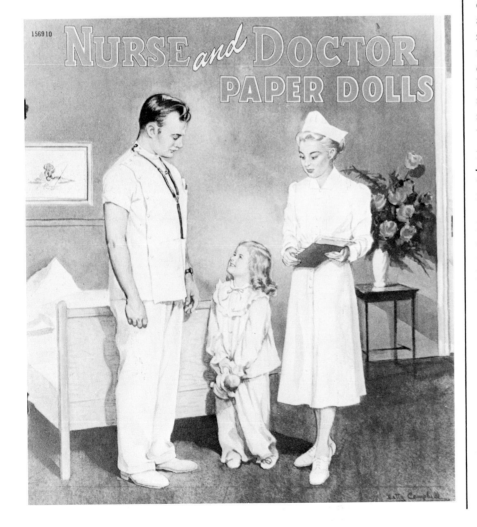

Louise Rumely understood paper-doll convention, creating paper-doll children of unsurpassed cuteness. "Watch Me Grow" has six adorable children aged one to six; 1944. (*Merrill Publishing Company*).

Sidney Sage's Peter Rabbit delighted children in the 1930s and keeps its charm today; 1934. (*Saalfield Publishing Company*).

A winsome pastel paper doll by Maud Tousey Fangel, Baby Bunting seems almost alive; Lowe, date unknown. (*Samuel Lowe Company, Inc.*).

Peggy came neatly boxed, eliminating the child's need to requisition shoe boxes or other containers. Her smiling face made her an ideal imaginary playmate; Spear Company, c. 1935.

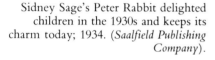

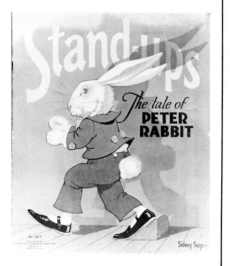

144

An offensive compendium of racist stereotypes, Patches and Petunia is, happily, a period piece; 1937. (*Saalfield Publishing Company*).

Louise Rumely studied fine arts in Chicago, and was a fashion artist before she opened a commercial art studio. Rumely specialized in the rounded babies and children that collectors seem to love most. The Swan Soap advertising of the 1940s, "Star Babies," "Cradle tots," and "Watch Me Grow" are typical of her easy-to-recognize style of illustration. Her sets command high prices on dealers' lists today.

A different tradition is represented by the work of artist Jeanne Voelz, who studied at Parsons School of Design and has had a studio of her own since 1952. Voelz drew all of the later Shirley Temple dolls for Saalfield, and specializes in celebrity dolls. Her sets include Sandra Dee, Susan Dey, Jane Fonda, Shari Lewis, Kim Novak, Marlo Thomas, and Jane Russell. Voelz also did the books based on Pat, Julie, and Tricia Nixon. Her work has a

Fascinatingly morbid, Deerfield paper dolls told the story of an Indian massacre. The little books included in the set gave accounts of the vanished children. It was one of the best story-and-picture sets of its time; (*Deerfield Academy*).

Milo Winter captured the allure of faraway places in these cutouts of Eskimos and Mexicans; Whitman, date unknown. (*Western Publishing Company, Inc.*).

Meine Käthe Kruse Püppen

pleasant realism that is easy to identify.

As a beginning collector, if you learn to know the work of these artists alone, you can collect a magnificent group of paper dolls. For people who like methodical ways, searching out and gathering the work of a single artist is a challenging hobby. Anyone who can amass

Kathe Kruse was one of the finest contemporary doll makers. Her single set of paper dolls, drawn from her own dolls, is most appealing; Germany.

all of a single great artist's work will own a valuable collection.

If searching out the work of a single artist seems too scholarly an ap-

These ballet paper dolls, bought to interest a ballet-loving daughter, formed the nucleus of the author's paper-doll collection twenty years later; Whitman, 1955. (*Western Publishing Company, Inc.*).

This enormous *pantin* was sent to the author after a lecture, by a Canadian friend; c. 1930.

An amusing twist on an old idea: "Slippery Faces" not only change costumes but also change faces; 1921. *Delineator, (Butterick Fashion Marketing Company)*.

Blackwell's Durham Farmyard is inhabited by beautifully drawn paper animals, including a regal peacock; U.S., c. 1895. A collection could be made solely of paper animals.

"The Model Book of Animals" features realistically drawn specimens, like the impressive elephant; McLoughlin, c. 1900.

A generation of children memorized Longfellow's "Hiawatha." Harold Cue made him a paper playmate in "Playmates from Storyland," 1922.

proach to paper-doll collecting, forget it. One of the fascinations of paper dolls is that there are many ways to enjoy them, and one can be found to suit your own particular taste even beyond categories like fashion or families. The paper dolls you will enjoy most are the ones which appeal especially to you. Recognizing this, most collectors I know have at least one album that defies all classification, except putting what most appeals to them in one place so it can be looked at again and again.

My own special favorites, based on such a nonsystem, are by artists good and less good, which cover a range of time and place. Their appeal is simply personal.

All collectors have favorites, and whatever yours are, go ahead and collect them. After all, paper dolls remind us of our own special pasts. This is often the happiest reason for collecting them.

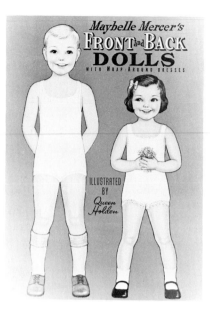

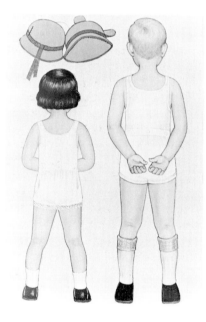

The appropriately named Dimple Triplets have no known background. Such mysteries keep collectors intrigued; U.S., date unknown.

Queen Holden's figures for Maybelle Mercer's "Front and Back Dolls," the only dolls in a modern commercial set printed on both sides, and a rare example of collaboration by two first-rate artists; Whitman, 1939. (*Western Publishing Company, Inc.*).

WHERE TO FIND PAPER DOLLS

Once you decide to collect, you suddenly find paper dolls everywhere, just as when you learn a new word, you discover it in everything you read.

Many women have saved one or two paper favorites from their own childhood or from their children's playthings. My own collection was based on a small number of both. Unlike bulkier toys, paper dolls are easy to tuck in a file, put in a bookcase, store flat in a bureau drawer. Somehow many are saved this way. Think hard; perhaps the start of your collection is in your house now.

Or perhaps it is in the home of a friend. Ask around. Lots of women have kept a few beloved paper-doll books or cut sets in an old envelope. Most will be pleased to let you feature their material in your collection, especially if you offer to catalog or label the dolls as a gift.

Paper dolls as a collection expand quickly, simply because few people consider them valuable. If you collected chairs or china, few friends would give you extras or bring you pieces from their travels. But paper dolls are so easy to keep and pack and so inexpensive to buy that most people will give you what they have because you promise their material a good home.

Your first step is to canvass friends and neighbors. My collection has mushroomed because even casual friends have handed over their family paper dolls or brought what they have found on their travels. Those gifts are happy reminders of their donors.

Your next step is to subscribe to a paper-doll magazine or newsletter. The main publications are listed in the Bibliography. These publications are managed by knowledgeable and dedicated collectors who are untiring about identifying material and sharing their news. Every

publication has articles about artists, kinds of paper dolls, histories, and illustrations of histories. All bring you news of buying and selling, conventions and parties in different cities, as well as information on mending, labeling, storing, and researching paper material.

It only takes a very few issues to become familiar with the names of other collectors. All issues contain the names and addresses of dealers with lists of paper dolls to sell. One subscription is a must for any collector or would-be collector. The costs of all the publications are low, never more than six or seven dollars a year. You may quickly find you want more than one, and you will be wise to save the issues for your own research.

The publications are chatty, informal, and highly practical. They are often illustrated, so you can compare your finds with pictures of known dolls. Nearly every collector began believing he or she was the only person in the world interested in something as trivial as paper dolls; all the publications are filled with letters from readers who have discovered they are not alone, and that an interest they have been half-ashamed to admit is actually a highly respectable and profitable hobby.

From the newsletters and quarterlies you will learn the names of the most important dealers. When you write to them, always include a self-addressed stamped envelope (SASE). You will then be in the group. The average lists of the large dealers are ten or more pages closely filled with hundreds of paper-doll buys. And there are always individuals wanting to sell or trade, with smaller lists. These will also be advertised in the publications, so you will never miss anything if you stay alert.

If you use the dealers to build a basic collection, you can also join in

the conventions and parties where buying and selling take place. You can go through actual material instead of lists, and decide what you want to buy, or learn about new paper dolls easily. You will also meet nearby collectors who will want to show you their collections and see yours. Learning spreads rapidly, and you will become an expert very fast. The parties feature all the challenge and haggling of any major exchange of valuables. The joy of trading your duplicate Shirley Temple for a Jane Withers you owned as a child can be highly satisfying.

Outside the paper-doll network you will find material at antique shows fancy and plain, flea markets, fairs, thrift shops, junk shops, rare-book dealers, secondhand book shops, and in almost any place where old things are sold. They may not always be displayed, so learn to ask and keep asking, surviving the stares from people who have none for sale. Always remember to shake out piles of old magazines and to investigate any kind of flat container. Valuable dolls have been found in old Bibles, among dress patterns, in knitting-instruction books, cigar boxes, and among all the paraphernalia of women from other times. The thrill of finding a European embossed royalty paper doll in an old ledger—and buying it for fifty cents from a dealer who never knew it was there—is unbeatable.

Knowledge is vital. You cannot find a treasure and keep it unless you have a notion that it is a treasure. Study the history of paper dolls, and keep your information and notes to look over for the moment when you have a mystery paper find. There is not that much material for you to learn, and there is a great deal you can contribute.

Aside from dealer lists, my main treasures have come from a friend who lives in England and enjoys looking for paper dolls when she shops for antiques; from a rare-book dealer who occasionally finds paper dolls hidden in books; and from friends who have admired my albums often enough to recognize good paper dolls when they find them here and abroad. The owner of a greeting-card shop once sold me a complete collection of the Boston *Herald* Ladies uncut, with several sheets no collector I asked had ever seen before. He apologized for asking fifty dollars for the set, although I could have sold it all for six times as much an hour later. Every collector who has rescued paper dolls from the Philistines has a similar story. If you know your turn will come.

HOW TO RECOGNIZE, IDENTIFY, AND DATE PAPER DOLLS

Your next step is to acquire one or more of the identification books and encyclopedias. They help you discover where a tiny hat belongs, how your cut dolls looked in their original uncut state, and how complete your set may be. Use them as stamp collectors use identification books, matching your find to the black-and-white illustrations.

Once you know some history, you have a general idea of how your paper doll fits in, whether or not someone else has found it and identified it precisely. The reference books help you know exactly what you have. They list paper dolls by title, date or approximate date, publisher, artist, and other criteria, depending on which ones you use.

Use what you already know. Examine the backs of your dolls; Tucks, for example, are always labeled. Magazine dolls will have printing or parts of pictures on the backs, and can be grouped by turning them over. Feel the paper and look at it through a magnifying glass. You can match sets by matching the paper on the backs, even without labels. Sometimes a child will have written names and even dates on a beloved set. Always look your paper dolls over carefully on both sides.

For example, suppose you buy a cut paper doll, a woman with two dresses and a hat. A glance tells you the approximate period of the costumes. An ankle-length skirt, a fussy blouse, and hip-hugging trumpet silhouette immediately suggest a 1930s look. Then look at the face and pose. Ideal beauty was stylized in each decade. If your doll has a demure, sweet expression, a tilted head, and tightly rolled hair, you know she belongs to the 1930s. If the hat is a cloche and close-fitting, you are in the early 1930s, because 1920s hats lasted into the early Depression years. Now turn your doll over; if the paper matches another doll, you have the start of a set. Look back, if the face is famous, identification is simple. If not, makeup styles will help pinpoint the period. Keep the memory of your doll in your mind as you read newsletters and references or look at other collections. The triumph when you spot your mystery doll is great. Once you know, label your find. You can then help others to know more; few fields let you start contributing to general knowledge as fast as paper-doll collecting.

Remember that only a handful of people know more than you do. The greatest paper-doll experts are women whose mothers were collectors or dealers, who grew up absorbing detail, and to whom paper dolls are old friends. But all are still learning. When you discover something no one of them has ever seen, you feel expert indeed.

I recently found the large Napoleon and Mary Queen of Scots dolls, (p. 112). Sense tells me they are Victorian, because they are pieces of English history, and in that era paper dolls often used historical subjects. I have four of the series. But no one knows how many more there were, or what subjects they covered. The publishers are unknown. Until someone finds a match and shares his or her information, the dolls remain a mystery.

This is why paper-doll experts develop tremendous visual memories. Collectors seem to remember a hundred different albums at once. They write, "You know that hat on the upper left of a page in the middle of your album? It belongs to a Lettie Lane set from 1910, and I think you have it cataloged wrong."

All the publications welcome pictures or descriptions of mystery dolls. Some reader usually writes back to make a good identification, or holds the picture in his mind until an identification is found.

You will also want a good history of costume. Find one that concentrates on the two centuries of paper-doll history. You will easily learn to match the bustle worn by your mystery paper doll to one from a contemporary print. This makes dating paper dolls easy, even for beginners.

Learn to check what you buy against the standard references. Take note of fashion, illustration style, printing techniques, the feel of the paper. It is easy to tell the difference between a 1940s dress with a short skirt, dull finish and matching veiled hat and a shiny, flimsy paper doll with part of a magazine article printed on its back, wearing clothing obviously from the 1920s. The more you look at pictures that have been identified, the easier it is to identify your stray finds.

An easy way to recognize, identify, and date a paper doll is to send it, or a copy, as a query to any of the publications. All of them offer this service to readers. A more satisfying way to do it is to research on your own.

For example, a handy way to date McLoughlins (for which thanks are due to Bart Anderson, director of the Chester County Historical Society in West Chester, Pennsylvania) is to check the folder addresses in New York City which correspond to the following years:

1854–1863	24 Beekman Street
1864–1870	30 Beekman Street
1871	52 Greene Street
1872–1886	71 and 73 Duane Street
1887–1890	623 Broadway
1891–1892	623 Broadway and 190 Mercer Street
1893–1898	874 Broadway
1899–1907	890 Broadway

Of course, if you find McLoughlins cut or without their folders, you cannot pinpoint the dates so easily. Many of these dolls were printed and reprinted, so dating is precarious.

Detective work like this is going on all the time among collectors, and each discovery is happily shared through paper-doll publications. You can benefit from these discoveries and go on to make your own.

HOW TO REFINE YOUR COLLECTION

There are approximately twenty great paper-doll collections in the United States. Several factors make them great. Each is large, covering the entire range of paper-doll history. Each has unique pieces, especially handmades of all periods. Each represents all categories of collecting; specialists find material in them as good or better than their own. These collections are slowly moving into museums, as people learn the social value of the material and the need for preserving it properly.

You can still build a fine collection, even if you cannot buy all the dolls you see (although paper dolls cost far less than most other material). Ingenuity and memory play a tremendous part in amassing paper dolls. Time is also a big factor. If you can spend part of every weekend looking around your neighborhood for finds, and part of every day arranging your material to see what you lack, money is far less important. If you are a willing correspondent, answer every ad and inquiry in the publications, and patiently track down the women in Iowa who has the single piece you need to complete your set of Clark's O.N.T. dolls, your collection can be excellent in a short time.

A few rules apply. Cut paper dolls are worth approximately half the prices of uncut. Mint condition is the standard for value. Complete sets are worth more than incomplete. This means that a lucky find of just one 1930s paper-doll book, uncut and in mint condition, can be worth a bunch of uncut and battered paper dolls in assorted bits and snippets.

The smartest collectors buy odd lots, batches, big boxes of mixed lots of paper dolls. They patiently sort the material, and they apply every ounce of knowledge to the work. They have assembled great collections because they could spot a Queen Alexandra in a junk shop, even mixed in with old bills, comic books, and matches.

Almost all collectors find their budgetary standards expand rapidly. When you collect $3 dolls, the idea of a $25 set is inconceivable. When you have reached the point of grabbing a Holden uncut book for $40, the thought of a Jenny Lind at $800 is beyond belief. But as you learn how easy it is to recoup, and to sell for more than you paid just by waiting a few months, you tend to become more adventuresome.

Every new issue of a paper-doll publication brings news of prices no collector would have believed only ten years ago. *Paper Doll Quarterly,* in its summer 1980 issue (mailed in January 1981, in the gentle fashion of paper-doll publications), lists advertising from a California dealer who wants to sell 1941 cut Alice Faye dolls for $90. Bette Davis dolls from 1942 were selling for $85. Both were originally a dime. I acquired both in a large lot a few years ago, probably for $10 apiece. At about the same time I was offered an eighteenth-century English paper doll of great magnificence for $1,000. I wish I had plunged. Today it cannot be had for less than $3,500.

To make your collection valuable, follow the rules. Buy as much as you can afford today. Prices are going higher as more people become interested, new collectors want particular dolls, and existing collections break up or are inadvertently destroyed. Buy dolls you want in their cut state, because their price will rise to the level of the complete book you cannot afford now. If you can, pick up any sets in mint condition or complete, even if you do not want, like, or need them. You will be able to use them as bargaining material to get something you do want desperately.

Keep a small notebook of pieces and sets you need to complete a series. Try to be in the right place at the right time, whether it is your local junk auction or one of the big New Hampshire paper-doll auctions where paper dolls sell for fortunes. Money, time, patience, care, memory, attention, and taking pains can all make a collection more valuable.

HOW TO GET RID OF PAPER DOLLS YOU NO LONGER WANT

The time will come when your cut Lettie Lanes, last year's treasures, are replaced by your find of a complete sheet, with several extra pieces you never knew about. You now have a duplicate. Far from being a problem, it is your ticket into the exciting world of trading and selling that is so much a part of paper-doll collecting.

Keep a careful lookout at other peoples' wants in the small ads in paper-doll publications. If someone particularly wants an item you have, you can get a better price or trade for it than if they are merely taking it off your hands.

You can advertise extras yourself. Hundreds of collectors wait until they accumulate batches of duplicates and then get into the mail-order business by advertising lists of their own for sale. The smallest paper-doll lists are read and used.

You can save your duplicates for a paper-doll party or convention in your area, where you can trade or sell them. Someone will want them; new collectors build basic collections all the time; and there are limits on the numbers of pieces and no limits on the numbers of newly interested people.

If you want to trade, offer number for quality or quality for number. Whether you want one handsome figure or a batch of unsorted dolls depends on you. Trades have the advantage of costing nothing, and most collectors are geared to this method of exchange.

If all else fails, organize a paper-doll party of your own. You may know a number of women and men who might be interested in beginning collections. Use your extra material to start others off.

PRICE OF PAPER DOLLS: YESTERDAY, TODAY, AND TOMORROW

Any price list in today's rapidly rising market for all antiques is out of date almost as it is published. A research job that remains for collectors of paper dolls is to chart well-known groups over the past years in order to appraise today's price and guess wisely at tomorrow's.

Between 1976, when I began collecting, and today, prices have soared. Every new paper-doll publication brings gasps of amazement at new prices. Your joy in the rising value of your collection is usually tempered by your sorrow at the cost of acquiring the precious dolls you especially wanted. Sheila Young cut paper dolls were going for about three or four dollars a set in 1976, and now sell for ten or eleven; Tuck

complete sets were about twelve dollars at that time, and now cost about thirty.

Some dealers charge slightly more than others, and you will quickly learn the best value by comparison shopping. But often a special situation will temporarily send a price down. A dealer will want to gather money for a special purchase, and will let things go more cheaply than usual. If you want to learn fast, keep a small list of a particular doll and see how the prices vary. The three-character version of *Gone with the Wind* sold uncut for a $100 in 1976, went to $200 in 1978, and now appears at $300 and more. *Little Fanny,* complete and in mint condition, sells today for more than

$400; but if you settle for an incomplete set and take your chances of finding the missing bits, you can buy one even today for about $200.

A famous paper doll known as the Protean Figure, sold in England in 1811 for one pound, one shilling. The figure comes in its own complex folder, and contains ninety pieces, twelve costumes per envelope, and a scenic background. The costumes include a monk's habit, a naval uniform, a mourning costume, a Hussar's uniform, a knight's armor, a gentleman's evening wear, and more. This fabulous paper doll was offered to me in 1979 for $1,000. I would not have dreamed of paying so much for any paper doll at that time. Today the doll, when it can be found, goes for almost $4,000. Every collector has a similar story.

A self-addressed stamped, envelope sent to three dealers who advertise in the first publication you look at will tell you today's story correctly. This is better than using any price guide, even one a few months old. Consider these following 1980 averages:

June Allyson, 1957, uncut	$ 32.50
Betty Hutton, 1951, uncut	40.00
Malibu Francie, 1973, uncut	5.00
Queen Holden All Size, 1945, uncut	40.00
Deanna Durbin, 1941, uncut	165.00
Sonja Henie, 1939, uncut	185.00
Ziegfeld Girl, 1941, uncut	250.00
Dolly Dingle sheet, 1922, uncut	14.50
Lettie Lane sheet, 1910, cut	7.00
McLoughlin Little Pet, cut	75.00
Little Fanny, 1811 edition, fair condition	500.00
Jane Arden newspaper doll, uncut	5.00
Buttermilk advertising doll	10.00
Gone with the Wind, three-character, incomplete, cut	275.00

Remember, however, that you can come across any of these books, even uncut, in a thrift shop, a neighbor's house, or even your own attic.

Imagine how you will feel if you do.

Collectors often hold auctions through the mails using sealed bids, and sometimes go into extra rounds if the bidding is brisk. One publication regularly serves as a clearinghouse for duplicates using the auction method. More valuable material is usually professionally auctioned; anyone can attend and bid, though the prices are often high. Again, the more time you can put in, the less money you will need to spend.

Orderly collectors budget for pa-per-doll purchases, watch the prices for bargain breakthroughs, and do not exceed their pocketbooks. Most people, however, stand ready to jump at a special bargain even if it costs more than they ought to pay. Risks are minimal. If you get stuck you can almost always resell, and if you hold, your paper dolls are almost sure to rise in price.

Be aware of merchandise offerings in your local newspaper. People who want to get rid of piles of old paper may give you a good price when you volunteer to cart it away.

Advertise on your own. Do it inexpensively in neighborhood or school papers, on bulletin boards in supermarkets or schools, at a church exchange bulletin, and even in classified ads, which cost a little. When you buy, you set the price. And you may make some surprising local discoveries, like the woman who found out her neightbor's attic was loaded with old dolls.

Whatever you pay for your paper dolls today, you can be sure they will be worth more if you keep them carefully. In the past few years no collector has had to wait more than a few months to get his money back or make a profit.

Care and Display

HOW TO PROTECT AND PRESERVE YOUR COLLECTION

Paper is aged by contact with air and spoiled by handling. The first rule is to get your paper treasures into some kind of protective covering. This can be as inexpensive as plastic food bags, or as elaborate as glass or plastic frames, and anywhere in between. All stationery stores have plastic envelopes in many sizes. These allow you to pore over both sides of your doll without actually touching it. Old and crumbling paper dolls are best placed in individual plastic envelopes. Cut dolls with many pieces do best mounted with stamp hinges on paper and covered with plastic wrap, so they are easily seen but will not slide about. Never glue dolls onto paper; never use adhesive tape to hold them; never do anything to harm them when they are picked up and removed to a different place in your collection.

The overwrap is the general rule. One day you may want to handle your doll, and nothing must keep you from being able to exam-ine it completely, front and back. Most collectors will not use adhesive tape even to bind plastic wrap. It has a way of making contact with the doll when you least expect it. Inexpensive plastic frames are excellent to display favorite dolls. The pressure of the frame holds the doll in place.

Since sizes vary from one inch to life size, paper dolls offer special storage problems. Most collectors keep like-size dolls in albums, but also have a bureau, file cabinet, or closet in which to wrap and store uncut books and boxed sets.

Albums with looseleaf-style acetate pages, which offer extra refill pages, seem to be favorites among all collectors. The covers hold labels, and the pages can be rearranged easily as you fill in missing pieces. My own collection which now has thousands of pieces, is housed in ten such albums arranged chronologically, with an extra three-drawer bureau for uncut books, boxes, and larger pieces.

Few collections could compress so much material into so small a space. Paper dolls are wonderful for apartment dwellers. If you live in a house, especially one with an attic or basement, you are very fortunate. Really lucky collectors have paper-doll rooms of their own. With the departure of my children I gained one, complete with tables, fluorescent lights, shelves for reference material, and files for publications. It has helped me enjoy my collection more, but I managed handsomely on the dining-room table for years before.

Use only pick-up adhesive labels to mount your paper dolls. The smallest Avery labels are excellent. Pinch them in half, stick one side to the doll and the other to a page, and you have a nonslide mount that can be picked up without a trace. Mounting cut dolls is important; unless they are properly mounted they can slip into the binding and be crushed.

First buy one album and one set

of sticky labels, and clear one small corner for your collection as it grows. One box of unsorted paper dolls, bought cheaply at a junk auction, can give you hours of pleasure as you sort and group and label according to your own fancy.

If you like being organized, buy index cards and catalog your collection as you go. You can list pieces by title, place of discovery, gift of so-and-so, known references, date of doll, date of acquiring, price paid, condition. You can attach photocopies to each card if you have the time and money to do so. Some collectors enjoy managing all this organization, but many simply pop their new finds into albums and enjoy looking them over. Suit yourself. Your albums can hold simple labels

or no information at all.

Try to keep a record of what you paid, if only to delight yourself. One of the joys of collecting is noting on a new-dealer list for ten dollars a doll that you bought last year for fifty cents.

You should also try to keep, if only in your head, a want list. Most collectors need particular pieces, or dream of finding particular sets. They tend to carry little notebooks everywhere, so they can make choices quickly when they see several things they want at once.

You often have to buy paper dolls under pressure. Say you are at a fair. A dealer kicks over a battered box of shredded paper. At first glance, you notice four tattered Betty Bonnets, a few crumpled Dolly

Dingles, three ugly newspaper dolls, one Princess Alexandra, and a few handmades you have never seen in any reference book. If the dealer asks fifteen dollars for the box, and you know you can sell Alexandra immediately for twenty-five, you will be tempted to buy the box and rush home to see if Prince Edward is somewhere at the bottom to complete the pair. But be cool and calm enough to offer ten dollars, and bargain.

If you have a ready system for sorting, mounting, and arranging your material and for protecting it against ever landing again in a crumpled box, you will no longer be a beginner, but a seasoned collector of paper dolls.

HOW TO MEND PAPER DOLLS

My own general rule is, don't. Paper-doll value comes from original condition. Any mend, however skillful, lowers the intrinsic value of an untouched piece of the past. But many collectors disagree. They patch hands and feet, reattach missing legs, re-create parts of dolls with their own artistry. Some add celebrity faces to ordinary dolls of the same period, carefully labeling them as their own creations. Others want complete dolls, covering over tattered figures with unbroken costumes.

If you want to mend, do it properly. Never use glue or anything that binds permanently, in case you ever want to restore your doll to its original state. Use tiny pieces of sticky labels which can be peeled off; work from the back, placing the tape on a flat surface and pushing your doll onto it from above.

A rule of honor among collectors is to tell prospective buyers what you have mended, and never to pass off a mended doll as perfect. As far

as I know this rule is religiously kept. When you have a few paper dolls of your own, you learn to spot mending quickly.

A crumbling paper doll that must be saved can be placed whole on a large peel-off label. This will keep it from utter destruction, and is a last resort.

What usually disappear on paper dolls are fingers, toes, feet, and hands, especially if the poses are outstretched or elaborate. The dolls from pre–transparent tape days often have white adhesive mends. Removing these usually makes things worse. Practice leaving dolls as you found them and you will not contribute to their further ruin.

Very skilled collectors carefully save the backs of doll folders or the envelopes used to store them, which are often contemporary with the dolls. Since the paper is the same age as the dolls, it makes the neatest repairs. Every mending situation is different, depending on the paper, age, dyes, finish, and fragility of

each paper doll. One collector plunges edges into boiling water and presses the softened paper fibers together for invisible—and nonpermanent—mends. Another chews the pieces, using saliva to bond the paper. It works.

You may be tempted to clean very old paper dolls. It can be done, using peroxide on a cotton swab, bleaching out the oxidation of the years, especially on white areas that have turned brown. It was recommended to me for any paper dolls which are greatly aged by contact with air. I never dreamed of trying, preferring the look of age to any possible "improvement" I could create. Furniture collectors often do not refinish mellowed wood to modern brightness, treasuring the look of time. The same principle holds for me, but collecting is an individual pastime, and your own ideas are as good as anybody's.

HOW TO DISPLAY YOUR PAPER DOLLS

Since there are really so few known paper-doll collections on display, perhaps you will want to show yours in your home, and help spread the collecting idea to others. Handmades are little paintings worth framing. Amusing paper dolls from your childhood, or of a favorite person, are interesting decorations, and you will find you learn more about each doll if it is on display for you to study. Not so incidentally, displaying your collection tells others it exists, and you may find friends and neighbors who will want to add to it without being asked.

The simple, inexpensive plastic box frames sold in variety and stationery stores make it easy to have a changing gallery of your favorites and new acquisitons. The dolls are easy to pop in and out, so you can shift them easily, and the pressure of the frames keeps the dolls from slipping without tape or glue. Try making a row of six or eight frames in a hall, or arrange a group of different sizes on a wall. Your doll will be protected and ready for company and comment.

A child's room is a perfect place to display attractive paper dolls. Children can grow up with good examples of illustration in their original form. If you have good handmades, you may want to frame them permanently, in dustproof matted standard-size picture frames for the adult areas of your home. Collectors also use glass-topped tables for display, changing the arrangements as they like. The material is safe but visible up close, which is an excellent arrangement for small dolls.

Shadow-box frames can allow for elaborate framing, with as much surrounding trim, such as dried flowers or ribbon, as you like. Turn-of-the-century women framed their costumed paper dolls, and yours can complement antique furniture handsomely. As your collection grows you will want to keep an eye out for attractive frames, particularly the old ovals or extra deep ones. A pair displaying a paper-doll set can be a striking decoration for any room.

Your less valuable dolls, or duplicates, particularly if they are modern and can be replaced, can be used for all sorts of decorative projects, just as paper dolls always have been. While the rule is not to destroy any doll by gluing it, you are bound to accumulate some material that is cheap, like the modern reproductions. Charming objects have been made by collectors and their children, such as little greeting cards, match covers, frames, bulletins, and simple pictures. Of course, paper material can be used for collages, boxes, screens, and picture books, lacquered over with modern fixatives just the way the Victorians did.

If framing is not for you, you may want to buy a handsome display album and keep it where guests can look through your pages. Collecting is always more interesting if you can share your finds. Like almost everything about paper-doll collecting, suit yourself. The material is everywhere, waiting for you.

The great museums of the world do not often display paper dolls, even old and beautiful ones. Space is in short supply, and paper dolls cannot compete with paintings and valuable objects in the public's taste.

Even when paper dolls are in a museum's collection, most curators seem happiest when the dolls are under plastic and stored away from light and handling. Paper dolls are hard to display, needing showcases or flat wall frames, which take up room and can only be seen by a few people at a time. Furthermore, paper dolls are tricky to fuss with and difficult for novices to catalog and keep intact. Even with the advances in photocopying, little has been done to get paper dolls displayed in museums.

Nonetheless, you can see some spectacular collections in America and Europe. Historical societies, toy museums, doll museums, and some ephemera collections all show paper, especially those institutions with astute curators. Collectors who travel report paper dolls in many small museums. They all say that asking helps, and that many curators are happy to bring out hidden collections, even allowing visitors to handle bits and pieces of precious paper.

The Museum of the City of New York has a superb group of paper dolls and toys. Its curator, John Noble, is an expert on the material, as well as many other kinds of dolls and toys. While part of the collection is often shown along with costumes or other exhibits, it has been gathered in one place for cataloging, and Noble is generous about showing it to anyone who writes ahead for permission to view it.

The collection is large and particularly rich in the embossed European royalty dolls that collectors prize. The pieces are complete, with each tiny helmet, sword, bonnet, sacque and tippet in place. This is a boon to collectors who have found one or two pieces of a set and cannot figure out where they belong. Almost all periods of history are represented in the museum's collection, and almost all are in excellent condition.

Noble especially values the many beautiful handmades in the collection. These are, after all, the most original and valuable artistically, little primitives of their times. One handmade group every collector should see is a wedding party made in 1858 to celebrate the marriage of one of Queen Victoria's daughters. Each piece has its own personality, done in pastel watercolor to follow prints and sketches of the real people. The set is large and faithful to contemporary details, with dolls and costumes wrapped in a contemporary newspaper account of the wedding, and even the Archbishop of Canterbury represented on paper.

Noble has given much thought to the display and preservation of the collection. He points out that paper dolls need flat protective showcases or framing; asked how best to display paper dolls, his instant answer was in Lucite sheets that show fronts and backs of the material. No museums have yet achieved this ideal display.

In a city rich with art treasures, the Museum of the City of New York is outstanding for its reverence of paper dolls. The Metropolitan Museum of Art reports "a small collection, mostly of cripples." The New-York Historical Society, which displays the ephemera, postcards, posters, games, and advertising material of earlier times, has few paper dolls. Nevertheless, the Metropolitan presented a brilliant ephemera exhibition recently, and the catalog that accompanied it, *American Ephemera* by Janet S. Byrne, is a treasure of related material that contains interesting paper-doll pictures. The Cooper-Hewitt Museum, now a part of the Smithsonian Institution, also has a small collection of paper dolls, including a beautiful Jenny Lind.

The Toy Cupboard Museum, 57 East George Hill Road, South Lancaster, Massachusetts is a remarkable private collection owned and managed by Herbert Hosmer, a descendant of John Greene Chandler. Hosmer will open the collection to anyone who writes. Many of the early American and European paper dolls in the museum are shown with the original engravings and art work that produced them. Hosmer is especially knowledgeable, having devoted much of his career to the preservation of the material. The collection now includes the carefully assembled paper toys of Wilbur Macey Stone shown at the Newark Museum in 1931 and 1932. The catalog for that show is now a collector's item, since it offered photographs of many beautiful old paper toys. Hosmer has a rare Fanny Elssler, the original watercolors for the 1830 *Fanny Grey,* and many other treasures.

The Chester County Historical Society of West Chester, Pennsylvania has acquired the collection of Bart Anderson, one of the finest in America. The museum is in the process of cataloging this collection for display. The Mary Merritt Doll Museum at Douglasville, Pennsylvania, Flora Gill Jacobs's doll museum in Washington, D.C., and many other small private museums of dolls and miniatures often display good paper dolls.

The Museum and Library of Maryland History in the Maryland Historical Society, in Baltimore, has a paper-doll collection of 120 pieces, which is open to the public.

Detroit's Children's Museum has a fine collection of paper dolls among its real doll displays.

The Falmouth Historical Society in Falmouth, MA has a group of paper dolls for visitors to see.

The Wenham Historical Association and Museum at 132 Main Street in Wenham, MA has an excellent collection of paper dolls, costumes and toy cut-outs, which they will show to visitors on request.

The James Whitcomb Riley Museum in Greenfield, IN displays the paper dolls of its curator Dorothy June Williams in an upstairs room. She has been collecting them over many years.

The North Texas State University's Historical Collection has Oriental paper dolls and commercial examples from the 30s and 40s for visitors who write or call them to give notice.

The DAR Museum in Washington, DC also has some fine examples of paper dolls on permanent view.

Two other large collections are being cataloged in 1981 on the East Coast. The Margaret Woodbury Strong Museum in Rochester, New York is due to open in 1982. Strong's private collection of hundreds of toys, dolls, and related materials includes a magnificent group of paper dolls which has been cataloged by experts. And a major private museum is also readying a large collection of paper material for the public.

These are the best-known collections in America, although new ones constantly come to light and are reported in the pages of paper-doll publications. Shows, fairs, and toy shops are bringing paper dolls out from storage and attics, so you can never tell when you may run into a collection. Henriette Zabin, a collector, reports "stumbling across paper dolls on the second floor of the Presbytere facing Jackson Square, in the Vieux Carré of New Orleans." The owner of the *Paper Doll Newsletter* has just opened a museum called The Paper Doll on Highway 50 in Folsom, California. Keep your eyes open for a collection near you. The Smithsonian Institution in Washington, D.C., has some paper dolls in its Division of Domestic Life. And a fine collection is at Kent State University, which owns the archives of the Saalfield Publishing Company of Akron, Ohio. There are file copies of many Saalfield paper-doll books, along with some original art work. Dean H. Keller, the curator, is generous about showing the collection.

A museum may have one or two paper dolls only, but they can be treasures. The University of Indiana at Bloomington has paper dolls handmade by the poet Sylvia Plath. The Williamsburg Restoration has in its files a fantastic paper family called the Guzzle Family. Pure eighteenth-century satire, this family consists of caricature figures of Mr. Guzzle, a Dry Salter Worth Seventy Thousand Pound, Sally Guzzle, Wife to Mr. Sampson Guzzle In Her Youth Esteemed Pretty, Timothy Guzzle Eldest Son Of The Guzzles That Would Be A Soldier, and young Dick, Intended For——. Both drawings and captions are lively representations of their age.

If you go to Europe, Denmark is rich in paper dolls, both in shops and museums. The Dansk Folke-museum and the National Museum have collections of Danish, German, and French paper art. What the Danes call *paklaedningsdukker* are much beloved, modern dolls are still sold in toy shops, and the reproductions sold in the museums are superb. Museum personnel in Copenhagen are quite helpful and knowledgeable on paper-toy material.

In France, a charming small museum in Poissy, the Musée du Jouet, 2 rue de l'Abbaye, has a doll and toy collection which includes some beautiful examples in paper, including some interesting chromolithographed advertising material. The curator, Jeanne Damamme, is generous about showing and explaining the collection.

Switzerland, where so much beautiful printing was done from the eighteenth century on, has the Museum für Volkerkunde, and the Schweizerisches Museum, both in Basel. There are paper dolls and toys as well as beautiful scraps, valentines, and the paper ornaments used for *Oblaten,* the traditional German Christmas cookies wrapped in decorative paper. Basel has many museums containing antique toys, trains, folk carvings, and other items that contributed to the designs on paper, and are a pleasure to compare with the paper works. In any German-speaking area, ask to see the *Ankleidepuppen.* The uncut sheets are *Bilderbogen,* the costumes, *Trachten.*

While all paper-doll collectors feel certain that many paper dolls remain in Germany, which was the home of so many beautiful designs, the only reported museum is the Niederrheinisches Museum in Kevelaer. The museum has one of the greatest toy collections in West Germany, and includes paper dolls in its displays.

Research and reporting is left for the new collector who travels. It is impossible that paper dolls do not remain in Strasbourg, where so many were printed; in Nuremburg, the toy center of Europe in former times; and in Czechoslovakia, Hungary, and Poland, where paper dolls were favorite toys for so many people. As the material becomes more valued, perhaps these collections will come to light.

To see a great many good paper dolls in a small area, you must go to England and Scotland. The Bethnal Green Museum on Cambridge Heath Road in London, which holds the major collection of children's material from all the major London museums, has paper dolls dating from the eighteenth century and many examples from the nineteenth. There is a magnificent *pantin* of a man playing a musical instrument, and the Fuller books are represented. There are also twentieth-century dolls, including English advertising dolls which are charming and unusual. The museum is filled with related wonders—dolls, costumes, doll accessories, wood and tin toys—and offers a true idea of all the toys of the past.

The Museum of London at the London Wall has one or two eighteenth-century paper dolls, as well as handmades from the same century, and some Bavarian examples that appear to be unique. There are also card puppets, paper characters, a German game that is based on trick paper, and other fascinations in paper.

The Museum of Costume in the Assembly Rooms in Bath has some beautiful paper dolls along with its magnificent clothes. The whole collection was newly arranged in 1979, and includes underwear, accessories, and many articles of costume not usually seen in museums. Any paper-doll collector could learn to place costumes correctly after one or two visits. The Sudbury Hall Col-

lection in Derby displays "penny plains," paper animals, paper-doll houses and other related toys. Included is a peepshow from the Great Exhibition of 1851, as well as a "ship of matrimony" in a comic paper rendition.

The County Museum at Hartlebury Castle, near Kidderminster, has a few paper dolls and toys that are not always on display but that can be shown on request. A great number of small museums in England also have some paper material, which will be open to visitors on request. Always ask; you may be the first to make a discovery you can report to the paper-doll publications. The Gunnersbury Park Museum in London, for example, has a wonderful collection of dolls and toys, but does not make claims for its paper dolls. However, the museum has unusual paper animals, a *pantin* not seen anywhere else, and a German construction game for a coffee party, which contains "6 children, 3 jackets, 5 hats, 2 umbrellas, 1 fur tippet, 3 plates, 2 jugs, 1 sugar bowl, 1 tray of cups, 1 cake, 6 chairs and 1 table." It is well worth the trip.

Pollock's Toy Museum at 1 Scala Street in London also makes few claims for its paper dolls, since its main collection is the beautiful toy theaters, with the copper plates from which they were produced, as well as Epinal cutouts, peep shows, panoramas, and paper ornaments. The whole collection is fascinating for anyone interested in antique toys.

The Worthing Borough Council Museum has handmade paper dolls from the nineteenth century, as well as those related games and toys like candlelight amusements and shadowgraphs, panoramas and peep shows, England loved in the nineteenth century. There is a Jenny Lind in its original box, in beautiful condition, and well worth a pilgrimage for a paper-doll collector.

In Scotland, the Museum of Childhood on the High Street in Edinburgh has a superb collection of dolls, penny toys, Punch figures, pantomime costumes, cigarette cards, Nuremburg carved figures, puppets, soldiers, and much, much more, as well as some early paper dolls. Patrick Murray is the author of the museum's handbook, a particularly excellent history of children's amusements.

Books

The most important books are the following:

Advertising Paper Dolls: A Guide for Collectors (1975) by Marta K. Krebs, 13628 Middlevale Lane, Silver Spring, MD 20906.

A Collector's Guide to Paper Dolls: Saalfield, Lowe, Merrill (1980) by Mary Young, Collector Books, P.O. Box 3009, Paducah, KY 42001.

Paper Dollhouses and Paper Dollhouse Furniture (1975) by Barbara Whitton Jendrick, 79 Parkridge Drive, Pittsford, NY 14534.

Paper Dolls and Paper Toys of Raphael Tuck & Sons (1970) by Barbara Whitton Jendrick, 79 Parkridge Drive, Pittsford, NY 14534

Paper Dolls and Their Artists, Books 1 and 2 (1975, 1977) by Mary Young, 1040 Greenridge Drive, Kettering, OH 45429.

Paper Dolls of Famous Faces, vol. 1 (1974) by Jean Woodcock, 5369 South Owasso, Tulsa, OK 74105.

Paper Dolls of Famous Faces, vol. 2 (1980) by Jean Woodcock, published by Hobby House Press, Cumberland, MD. 21502.

A Picture Book of Paper Dolls and Paper Toys (1974) by Barbara Whitton Jendrick, 79 Parkridge Drive, Pittsford, NY 14534.

Also important for collectors are the following, which reprint material uncut:

Dolly Dingle Identification Book (1971) by Joan Carol Kaltschmidt, 75–19

162 Street, Flushing, NY 11366.

Lettie Lane Identification Book and *Betty Bonnet Identification Book* (1972) by Helen Mouck, 840 Fischer Street, Glendale, CA 91205.

Two older books are also valuable for serious collectors. Both have been out of print for many years and appear on dealers' lists at exceedingly high prices. There are reports that both are to be reprinted.

Paper Dolls: A Guide to Costume (1951) by Clara Hallard Fawcett, published by H. L. Lindquist Publications.

Those Fascinating Paper Dolls (1965) by Marion Howard.

With these books, you will be well on the way to knowing, in detail, all that is known about paper doll history. All are available either from their authors or from dealers' lists, also readily available in the quarterlies and newsletters. If you are very lucky, your local public library may have copies of some. Some of these books are still being issued in sections, as the authors gather new material. The publications will keep you aware of new identification books and encyclopedias as they come out.

An amazingly detailed and professional publication lists every book, section of book, pamphlet, newspaper or magazine article, periodical, and yearbook concerned with any paper-doll subject:

"Paper Dolls: A Bibliography" (1976) by Virginia A. Crossley, 685 Canyon Road, Rochester, MI 48063.

In addition to the paper-doll references, the following books have provided much of the information:

Centuries of Childhood (1962) by Philippe Aries, published by Knopf.

Critical History of Children's Literature (1953) by Cornelia Meigs, Anne Eaton, Elizabeth Nesbitt, and Ruth Hill Viguers, published by Macmillan.

Discovering Toys and Toy Museums (1971) by Pauline Flick, published by Shire Publications Ltd., Cromwell House, Church Street, Princess Risborough Aylesbury, Bucks, HP179AJ, England.

Dolls (1974) by Kay Desmonde, published by Crescent (Crown).

The Juvenile Drama, (1977), The Museum of the City of New York.

People's Chronology (1979) by James G. Trager, published by Holt, Rinehart & Winston.

Paper-Doll Periodicals

Matchmaker, 6931 Monroe, Hammond, IN 46324.

Midwest Paper Doll and Toy Quarterly, Box 131, Galesburg, KS 66740.

Paper Doll and Paper Toy Quarterly Bulletin, 3135 Oakcrest Drive, Hollywood, CA 90068.

Paper Doll Gazette, Route 2, Princeton, IN 47670.

Paperdoll Newsletter, P.O. Box 586, Carmichael, CA 95608.

BB of Spain comes with a complete wardrobe for all seasons; Barcelona, c. 1965.

er dolls wear
l as they are
ity, 1964.

n of Mexico makes
st with the real
s move from side
l is moved, and
ed to be
Doll, date

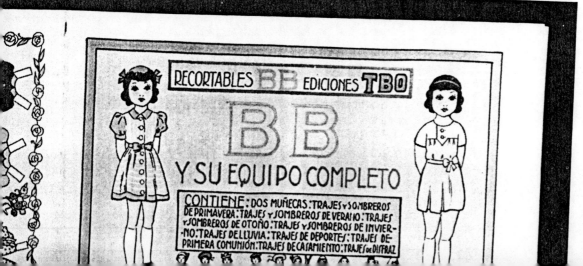

The Dane
in preservi
paper dol
C
beaut
dolls (*ab*
collect

nal outlay
per doll ex
one will b
for the pri
er fields
new colle
fooled by
painting f
experts ar
much safe

Thoug
seums hav
in their c
Copenhag

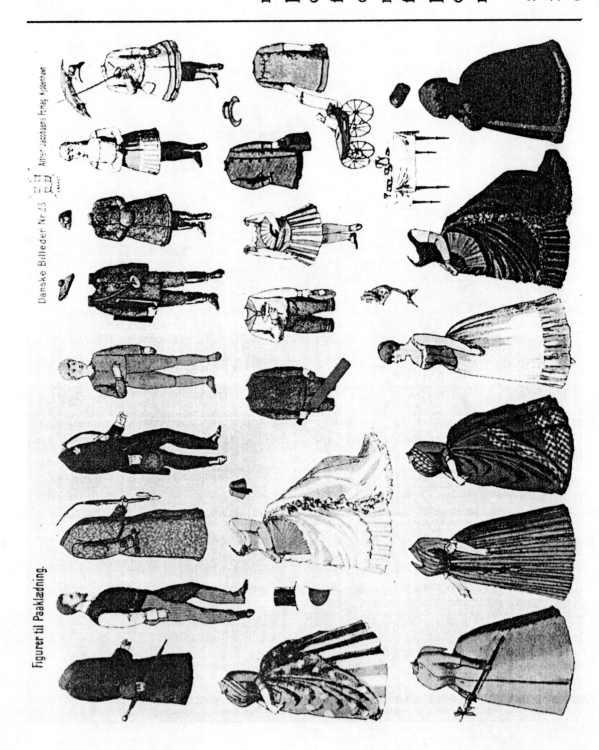

Danske Billeder Nr 23   Albert Jacobsens Forlag Kjøbenhavn

Figurer til Paaklædning.

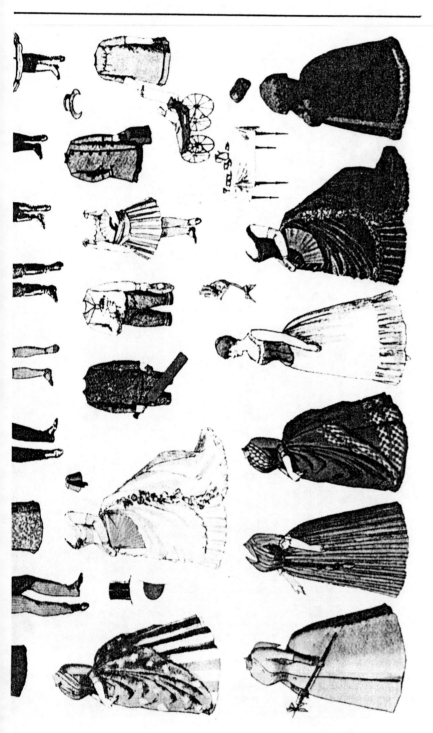

nal outlay to reproc
per doll exactly. Th
one will be able to
for the price of an or
er fields offer so
new collectors. Ex
fooled by furnitur
painting forgeries.
experts are more e
much safer.

Though compara
seums have reprodu
in their collections
Copenhagen Natior